THE GOSPEL ACCORDING TO
ST. MATTHEW

NEW TESTAMENT FOR SPIRITUAL READING

VOLUME 1

Edited by

John L. McKenzie, S.J.

THE GOSPEL ACCORDING TO ST. MATTHEW

Volume I

WOLFGANG TRILLING

CROSSROAD · NEW YORK

1981
The Crossroad Publishing Company
575 Lexington Avenue, New York, NY 10022

Originally published as *Das Evangelium nach Matthäus 1*
© 1965 by Patmos-Verlag
from the series *Geistliche Schriftlesung*
edited by Wolfgang Trilling
with Karl Hermann Schelke and Heinz Schürmann

English translation © 1969 by Herder and Herder, Inc.
Translated by Kevin Smyth

Library of Congress Catalog Card Number: 81-68164
ISBN: 0-8245-0110-1

PREFACE

I read once that the words of Jesus are quoted more frequently according to Matthew than according to any other gospel; and the main reason for this is simply that Matthew is the first of the gospels and therefore the one most likely to be read and to be consulted. For hundreds of years it was thought that Matthew was the first of the gospels in time as well as in arrangement; this is no longer maintained, but it was also a reason for quoting the earliest of the gospels as the model after which the others were written. But Matthew has other merits which still make it the most quotable gospel. We recite the " Lord's Prayer " and the beatitudes according to Matthew, although Luke has both of them. More than Mark and Luke, but less than John, Matthew constructs the sayings of Jesus into discourses, of which the Sermon on the Mount is the most celebrated. The chief merit of Matthew is that it is the most carefully written of the four gospels. When a saying of Jesus appears in two or three gospels, it is almost without exception true that the saying has a lapidary quality in Matthew which the other gospels less often achieve.

Matthew is the earliest document of the New Testament to exhibit an interest in the sayings of Jesus. Mark, the earliest gospel, contains few sayings. Luke and John, both later than Matthew, show the same interest in the sayings of Jesus. Paul, whose letters are earlier than Matthew, quotes Jesus no more than two or three times. To modern readers it seems strange that the early church, the generation of the disciples, should have shown so little interest in the sayings or the teaching of Jesus. Commentaries on other books will explain where the primary interest of the early disciples lay. Possibly Matthew was the earliest to develop an interest in the words of Jesus, and the reasons why he developed the interest deserve attention.

Matthew has often been called the most Jewish of the gospels, a description which must be used with reservation; he is less sympathetic to the Jews than Mark or Luke, more sympathetic than John. He is Jewish in the sense that the gospel was written for Jewish Christians, and apparently as an aid for conversation with their fellow Jews. Matthew presents Jesus as the Messiah of the Jews, the one promised and predicted in the Old Testament, a new Moses whose first proclamation is uttered on a mountain, the founder of a new Israel. Some commentators even find a division of the gospel into five parts corresponding to the five books of Moses. Hence Matthew's interest in the Old Testament, particularly as a document which is " fulfilled " in Jesus. He presents the Messiahship of Jesus as a transparent reality which is unseen only by those who refuse to see it. He is better acquainted with Jewish beliefs and observances than Mark and Luke, and more concerned with making the position of Jesus towards these beliefs and observances clear. Jesus did not come to destroy the law but to fulfill it.

Judaism of New Testament times was a religion of the law, the five books of Moses, even though the temple still stood as the sole legitimate place of sacrificial cult. The tradition of the law went back several centuries, and the teaching and observance of the law was much more meaningful to Jews than the sacrificial worship. Matthew clearly presents those whom he calls " scribes " and " Pharisees " as unfaithful interpreters of the law. Jesus is the one true interpreter. The Messiah could not be presented as one who had no teaching. Jesus is the fulfillment of the law; he is also the fulfillment of the teaching. Matthew presents the teaching of Jesus as the answer to the teaching of the scribes and the Pharisees. The Jewish Christian does not give up law and teaching, but receives them in their fullness. Matthew describes Jesus as using rabbinical language and engaging in rabbinical discussion more than the other evangelists. He is surely faithful in this feature to the historical Jesus, who was called " Rabbi " and accepted the title. But Matthew was also more familiar with rabbinical methods and techniques than the other evangelists.

Matthew does not believe that the law endures. The law must yield to its fulfillment. Jesus is the new Moses who founds a new Israel; he is also the proclaimer of the new law. This term must be used carefully, for it is not a New Testament term. What Jesus proclaims is not another law, but an entirely new and higher revelation. Jesus proclaims the gospel, which is in the new Israel what the law was in the old Israel, the authentic speech of God through the one who is sent. Like the law, the gospel reveals a new form of life. The sayings and discourses of Jesus in Matthew are principally concerned with questions of morality. The Sermon on the Mount contains a series of sayings called the " Antitheses," in which the law and its traditional interpretation are contrasted with the new morality proclaimed by Jesus. In each antithesis the standard of conduct is raised to a more demanding level: not only murder, but hatred is prohibited; not only adultery, but unchaste desires; divorce is rejected; not only perjury, but untruthfulness; not only revenge, but even self-defense; and the series culminates in the love of one's enemies. The same type of antithesis appears in other sayings of Jesus throughout the gospel. The law established standards of conduct; Jesus proclaims a morality of the heart.

This interest in the teaching of Jesus no doubt reflects a broader concern than the apologetic of Jewish Christians for their belief. It must have been early that the question was asked: What does it mean to be a Christian? How does a Christian live differently from other men? The first place to seek an answer was to ask what Jesus had said, and then to collect his sayings. Interpreters of the gospels believe that they can detect in some of the sayings the question to which the saying was an answer. To illustrate, divorce was permitted in both Judaism and Roman law. Is it permitted to a Christian? The saying of Jesus answers the question with an uncompromising negative. K. Stendahl has compared the author or authors of Matthew to Christian scribes, who drew up the sayings of Jesus as a guide to conduct much as Jewish scribes formulated a code of conduct on the basis of the law.

This emphasis on the teaching gives the Messiahship of Jesus the peculiar character which it has in Matthew; for no single New Testament writer ever recapitulated the fullness of the Messiahship. For all of them Jesus saves from sin. Matthew emphasizes salvation from sin through a new revelation which teaches man how he should avoid sin. Certainly the theme is not peculiar to Matthew, but the emphasis is. Matthew is as aware of the redeeming death and resurrection as Paul is; but Paul, as we have remarked, does not present Jesus as a teacher.

The reader of Matthew, if he takes the time to read slowly and thoughtfully, will find that the revolutionary character of Christian morality emerges with a clarity which can be disturbing. Unless he permits himself to be distracted by the ancient evasion that Jesus came to enunciate some impossible and impractical ideals, he will be compelled to ask questions about how Christian morality is to be realized in his life in this world. He will find the answers difficult but not obscure; indeed he may wish that they were more obscure. It is the merit of Matthew's lapidary style that evasion becomes impossible. This is the light that shines most clearly in Matthew, the light which cannot be covered.

John L. McKenzie, S.J.

INTRODUCTION

The word " gospel " which we know so well means originally
" good news," a message of joy. Primarily it is the message about
God which Jesus Christ delivers. But that could have been said
about the men of God in the Old Testament, especially the
prophets. There is more here. God speaks in a unique way, because through Jesus he says his " last word," to which he adds
nothing more. But above all, this message is incomparable, because he is his Son. He is the living Word of the Father, made
flesh, speaking not only by word of mouth, but by his whole
existence, his life and work. Thus " gospel " is at once good tidings about God and about Jesus Christ himself.

The Old Testament, the history of the people of God under
the ancient covenant, moves in wave after wave towards the salvation of God. Like the ebb and flow of the tide, this history is
mysteriously set in motion by the invisible God who works so
mightily. It is not, however, a constant return of the same thing,
a uniform rhythm of apostasy and conversion, wrath and grace.
It presses forward with an inward force, as in the pangs of birth,
towards the full revelation, the perfect salvation, the unity of
God and people. " You shall be my people and I will be your
God " (Ezek. 36:28). All longing is concentrated, ever more in-
tensely as the day draws nearer, upon the one promised saviour,
the Anointed, the Messiah. He shall perform the final task, join
his people to God, for the blessing of Israel and of all peoples.
More than any other Gospel, Matthew shows that the history of

the people culminates in the work of Jesus, that this Jesus of Nazareth is truly he whom the people awaited.

The divine history has been committed to writing section by section in the books of the Old Testament. They mirror it and disclose its divine meaning. On nearly every page, the scriptures manifest that inner impulse of history which moves on to a radical finality. They show above all how the figure of the Messiah takes on clearer and clearer outlines. The belief that *Jesus* is the Messiah puts everything in a new and clear light. Jesus is seen and interpreted through the eyes of the Old Testament. It is an immensely rich world that we enter: not the record of dry historical facts, not the biography of a great man, but the whole of history which God has brought about since the beginning of the world, and to which, in Christ, he said the " Yes " and " Amen " (see 2 Cor. 1 : 19f.). This is the way we must read the many passages where the evangelist points to the fulfillment of a particular Old Testament saying, or refers in general to some word or event of the ancient covenant.

A rich picture is drawn of Jesus the Messiah. Jesus is a prophet like the ancient prophets, the last in the series. His message is God's summons, a call to repentance, and a pledge of God's mercy (4 : 17). He also suffers the fate of the ancient prophets. He is misunderstood, contradicted, persecuted and even killed. He is the *teacher* of the people. He does not merely challenge a certain hour and situation with a word of decision. He also teaches the true way of justice (5 : 20). He sits down like the scribes giving a lecture (5 : 1); he uses the language of the Wisdom-teacher; he gathers round him a group of disciples. The framework of the Gospel of St. Matthew consists of great discourses of the Lord, which can be precisely described as pieces of instruction. In ordered sequence and clear articulation, the themes of the divine instruction are summed up there. He is the Servant of God, on whom God has laid his Spirit that he may proclaim the word of God and lead to victory. He follows obediently the will of the heavenly Father, and does good quietly and humbly: he heals those whose hearts are broken and whose bodies are sick and in misery. The crushed reed he does not break, and the flickering wick he does not quench (see 12:18–21); meekly he enters the holy city on an ass (21:5). Through lowliness his way leads to exaltation. He is the Son of God in a unique sense. Earlier, the king or even the whole people had been occasionally given this title. But never could anyone have said: " No one knows the Son but the Father, and no one knows the Father but the Son, and he to whom the Son chooses to reveal him " (11:27). He who underwent the deepest disgrace has been exalted by God to the highest dignity: " All power in heaven and on earth " has been delivered to him (28:18).

In the work of Jesus, not only is the past definitively revealed, but the history of Israel brought to its goal: the new thing is also contained in him, the true people of God from all nations. The birth of the new age is a birth of the whole world. In Jesus Christ is comprised the salvation of all peoples and ages. Its bearer is the people of the Messiah, the church. Sprung from a tiny seed, the circle of the disciples, it now bears the destiny of the world: the good news, the source of grace and the authority of the exalted Lord. " Go therefore and make disciples of all nations, baptizing them in the name of the Father and of the Son and of the Holy Spirit, teaching them to observe all that I have commanded you " (28:19f.).

Thus this " history of Jesus " gives at once the key to the ancient covenant and the new. It shows how deeply one are Christ and the church, the true people of God and the church.

We cannot read the gospel like a story book which merely re-counts some events of the past. We have no need to " translate " the word from the past into the present, or to work out artificially an application to our own life. The word addresses us, because it is the word of the church still living today, and most pro-foundly, because Jesus Christ himself utters this word through the church.

The object of this word is not to give a narrative, but a sum-mons. It desires to seep into the depths of our hearts and feelings like refreshing dew, fertilizing and quickening our finest forces. And above all, it wishes to be born of us in act. Thus the word of the gospel is the " Word of Life " in a twofold sense. It en-genders life in us because it is the holy and healing word of God. And through our actions, done according to the word, it is born again to life, to the glory of the Father in heaven and as a testi-mony for mankind.

OUTLINE

THE GOSPEL ACCORDING TO
ST. MATTHEW

PRELUDE TO THE HISTORY OF THE MESSIAH
(1—2)

Like St. Luke, St. Matthew begins his gospel with a prelude, but the two gospels are very markedly different from one another both in their style and in the events narrated. St. Luke gives us copious narratives in strong relief, while in St. Matthew we have succinct episodes, highly condensed for a theological purpose. At the beginning comes the genealogy of Jesus Christ (1 : 1–17), the first proof of Messiahship. A series of shorter sections follows (1 : 18—2 : 23), where only the adoration of the Magi (2 : 1–12) is given a more extensive description. Taken together, these sections form a continuous narrative whole as far as the transfer to Nazareth. The style is strikingly sober, almost like a chronicle. Peculiar to each section are the references to the fulfillment of Old Testament prophecies. These "fulfillment citations" are, as it were, the scarlet thread which is spun into the tissue and which has only one object: even the early events in the life of the Messiah have been miraculously arranged by God and agree with the Old Testament expectation.

The Genealogy of Jesus Christ (1:1-17)

The portal of St. Matthew's work is built of mighty blocks of well-hewn stone. A register of the generations, a family tree,

3

leads down through the centuries to the fullness of time. Since the return from the exile in Babylon, such family registers were highly prized by the Jews. During the racial intermingling of these centuries, Jewishness was maintained with fierce effort. It was, of course, a particular honor to belong to one of the ancient noble families, and especially to be connected with a branch of the royal family, which began with David. For this family was in fact the bearer of the promise. From it the royal scion was awaited, who was not only anointed like previous kings but was called simply " the Anointed," Messiah.

¹*The book of the genealogy of Jesus Christ, the son of David, the son of Abraham:* ²*Abraham was father of Isaac, Isaac was father of Jacob, Jacob was father of Judah and his brothers.* ³*Judah was father of Perez and of Zerah by Tamar, Perez was father of Hezron, Hezron was father of Ram.* ⁴*Ram was father of Amminadab, Amminadab was father of Nahshon, Nahshon was father of Salmon.* ⁵*Salmon was father of Boaz by Rahab, Boaz was father of Obed by Ruth, Obed was father of Jesse.* ⁶*Jesse was father of David the king.*

King David was father of Solomon by the former wife of Uriah. ⁷*Solomon was father of Rehoboam, Rehoboam was father of Abijah, Abijah was father of Asa.* ⁸*Asa was father of Jehoshaphat, Jehoshaphat was father of Joram, Joram was father of Uzziah.* ⁹*Uzziah was father of Jotham, Jotham was father of Ahaz, Ahaz was father of Hezekiah.* ¹⁰*Hezekiah was father of Manasseh, Manasseh was father of Amos, Amos was father of Josiah.* ¹¹*Josiah was father of Jechoniah and his brothers at the time of the deportation to Babylon.*

¹²*After the deportation to Babylon, Jechoniah was father of Shealtiel, Shealtiel was father of Zerubbabel,* ¹³*Zerubbabel was*

father of Abiud, Abiud was father of Eliakim, Eliakim was father of Azor. [14]*Azor was father of Zadok, Zadok was father of Achim, Achim was father of Eliud.* [15]*Eliud was father of Eleazar, Eleazar was father of Matthan, Matthan was father of Jacob.* [16]*Jacob was father of Joseph, the husband of Mary, of whom was born Jesus who is called Christ (Messiah).* [17]*So all the generations from Abraham to David are fourteen generations, and from David to the Babylonian captivity are fourteen generations, and from the Babylonian captivity to the Messiah fourteen generations.*

The conception and birth of Jesus took place by a unique miracle. We read about it in the next section. Was the effect of this miracle that Jesus stood quite apart from the natural bonds of family and nation, as though sent only by God into our world and our history, like a comet cutting through the atmosphere of the earth? Not at all! Through St. Joseph, who is legally his " Father," he enters into the series of generations. By this, sacred scripture testifies primarily that he is a *true man*; not one of those heavenly beings of whom the myths speak, which come down from heavenly regions and become visible on earth, to return then once more into the spiritual and heavenly world. Jesus is truly " born of a woman " (Gal. 4:4).

But further: the family in which he appears at a certain stage is a royal family, the house of David, the bearer of the messianic promises. Therefore, the first attribute given to Jesus Christ is Son of David. This is a bold description. Jesus is, in the full meaning of the word, and with legal right, a descendant of David, member of the royal family and heir to his throne (see 2 Sam. 7:1-16; Lk. 1:32). Could he have also been Messiah without this parentage? We do not know the answer, because

God so disposed events that his eternal Son " was of the seed of David according to the flesh " (Rom. 1 : 3). One thing is certain : if the proof could not have been given that Jesus was of the house of David, it would have been very hard for the Jews to believe that this Jesus could be the Messiah.

The second attribute has a still wider scope: *Son of Abraham.* It is not only the royal line which culminates in Jesus. More than the promises of the throne and enduring lordship are fulfilled in him. The list of ancestors is taken back in a wide sweep as far as Abraham. Abraham is the progenitor of the whole people, not only of one tribe. Above all, Abraham is the bearer of the still more ancient and far-reaching promise: " I will bless those that bless you, and I will curse him who curses you; and by your name shall all nations of the earth wish blessing on themselves " (Gen. 12 : 3). The people springing from his loins are to be a blessing for all mankind. They bear the blessing down through the centuries like a precious gift, till it concentrates itself in the one unique scion of the clan, who brings this blessing to all the world. " Now the promises were given to Abraham and his seed. He does not say, ' and to his seeds,' as though they referred to many, but as though referring to one only, he says, ' and to your seed,' who is Christ " (Gal. 3 : 16). From the ancestor of Israel the arch of history is spanned to the ancestor of a new Israel.

The genealogy of the evangelist from Abraham to Joseph is not complete. Many links are omitted. The sources from which it is put together are also only partly known to us. The first two sections, up to the Babylonian captivity, are undoubtedly derived from the biblical texts. The sources of the names given in the third section are entirely unknown. And it is not possible to test the accuracy of the genealogical tree. Finally, it ends rather strangely, not with Mary, who was after all the actual mother of

Jesus, but with Joseph, who was husband to her only according to law. All this helps us to understand this text. If Jesus was the legal son of Joseph, he could thereby be inserted into his list of ancestors in the full sense, and so into the descendants of David. St. Matthew does not give as much weight to " scientific " exactness as to the intrinsic order and consequence. This order is clearly indicated in the final verse, 17 : in each case, fourteen generations fill up the three intervals between Abraham, David, the Babylonian captivity, and Christ. Fourteen is twice the sacred number, seven. In the same numbers, there is revealed to the believing mind something of the order and plan of God in history. The birth of Jesus stands in a sacred context; it has been intended by God down through centuries and generations; and it took place precisely at the preordained time. For the evangelist and for his readers, this discovery is an indication of God's wise government of history.

Twice in the last verses the Messiah is mentioned with emphasis. Of Mary was born Jesus " who is called Christ," and " from the Babylonian captivity to the Messiah there are fourteen generations." The real object of the list of ancestors is to prove the true messiahship of Jesus! The first page of the gospel gives expression to what the whole book teaches from end to end: Jesus is truly the promised Messiah. On the other hand, the genealogy is traced to Abraham. Is this not already an indication that the Messiah must not be looked upon merely as a scion of the royal race and Son of David, and hence above all as a political figure? He comprises in his person all the promises, not only those that hold good for a chosen " dynasty," but those which are for a whole divinely consecrated people. From the very start, the image of the Messiah is too great to be exhaustively contained in the royal succession. Here it is a matter of the call and the mandate of Israel and of blessing or curse for the whole world. For him who knows that this Jesus is the Messiah the history of the whole world until his coming can be read as a meaningful plan of God, rich in promise.

The Events of the Birth and Childhood of Jesus (1:18—2:23)

The Birth of Jesus (1:18-25)

[18]*The birth of Jesus Christ was as follows. When his mother Mary had been betrothed to Joseph, before they came together it was found that she was with child by the Holy Spirit. *[19]*Her husband Joseph, being a just man and not wishing to have her disgraced, decided to divorce her secretly.*

This section tells of the birth of the Christ child. The way it took place is remarkable from many points of view. If we compare it with the nativity story with which we are familiar from St. Luke, its soberness and brevity are striking. The immediate circumstances, the preparations for the event, and the event itself are hardly presented at all. St. Matthew's attention is directed to completely different things. He takes it for granted that we are acquainted with the process of the miraculous conception and birth. They are recalled in only a few brief words. What is the main thing which the evangelist wishes to teach?

Everything is observed from the standpoint of Joseph. Indeed, at the end of the genealogy he had been mentioned as the " husband of Mary." The narrative of the birth links up with this. Mary was betrothed to Joseph and thereby, according to Jewish law, was looked upon as his legal wife. But still they had not yet " come together." This means that Joseph had not yet introduced his promised bride into his house, and had not yet begun the union of married life. But the narrative says very curtly that this was the time when it appeared that Mary was blessed with child. Clearly, Joseph himself had recognized the fact. What he does not know, the evangelist tells us at once in an anticipatory explanation, is that the child that lives in her is from the Holy Spirit. Nothing is said of the bewilderment, the anxiety and brooding, the doubts and wavering of the husband. We are not told what goes on in his mind and brings his decision to maturity. We learn only that he decides to separate in utter silence from his betrothed. The shame which he thinks has come upon her shall not disgrace her before all the people.

The attitude of Joseph in which his deliberations and his convictions find expression is described as " just." The just man is he who fixes his mind on God and arranges his life according to God's will, who fulfills the law joyfully and wholeheartedly. However, he also is just who is wise and kind, in whose life the experience of God's law and his own human maturity have been admirably mingled and illuminated. This is the Old Testament picture of the just man. He is the ideal of the man who is well-pleasing to God. Joseph cannot penetrate the bewildering riddle. But he does not search into it, or try to explain it.

[20]*But as he was considering all this, behold, an angel of the Lord appeared to him in a dream and said: " Joseph, son of David, do not be afraid to take to you Mary your wife. For the child that has been conceived in her is of the Holy Spirit."*

Only after the decision to separate has been made does God intervene. An angel, the holy messenger of God, initiates him into the mystery. He addresses him solemnly: " Joseph, son of David." Jesus is the only other person on whom this honored title is bestowed (Mt. 1:1; 9:27; 20:30f.). The words ring with the hopes which have been attached to this name since the prophecy of Nathan to the king: " I will be to him a father, and he shall be to me a son. When he does wrong I shall chastise him with a human rod and with human blows. But I shall not withdraw my steadfast love from him, as I withdrew it from Saul, whom I removed from your path. But your house and your kingdom shall be established before me forever; your throne shall abide for evermore " (2 Sam. 7:14–16). With this address the simple man Joseph is drawn into the context of divine history. He is a descendant of the race of David, one of his " sons "! What he hears from the angel, he must hear as a son of David. Then understanding will dawn on him; for we read that after the message in the night, Joseph acts obediently as the angel had charged him to (1:24).

21" *She will bring forth a son, and you shall call his name Jesus; for he shall save his people from their sins.*"

The messenger now expresses himself more clearly. Mary will bear a son and Joseph will give him the name " Jesus." It was the privilege of the father, and his rightful dignity, to give the child its name. It is, as it were, a creative act, since for the ancients the name signified the essence and the calling. But in the case of Joseph, this right is restricted. Not only has he no share in the begetting of the child, he has also no right to determine the name. It is given from on high, it is allotted to him beforehand; it is a name which had indeed often been used in the history of the people, but the nature of which had never been announced so precisely as here.

What does the name "Jesus" mean? Translated from the Hebrew it means that God is salvation, God is helper and saviour, God is redeemer. It was the name of Joshua, who, as successor of Moses, led the people over the Jordan into the sedentary life and the peace of the promised land. The name was borne by a high priest who, after the return home from the Babylonian captivity, took part in the reëstablishment of the cult and the service of the temple (Ezra 2—5). A teacher of wisdom, who could praise the way of justice and life in well-made sayings, had the same name, Jesus, the son of Eleazar and the grandfather of Sirach, author of the book of Jesus ben Sirach (Ecclesiasticus 50:27). All in different ways were mediators of God's salvation. But Jesus is to bring this salvation in a comprehensive way, as did no one before him. This is implied by the interpretation of the name which St. Matthew adds: "He shall save his people from their sins." It is not just the blessing of a fruitful land, of a sacrificial service pleasing to God, or of right knowledge. It is liberation from an enslavement more profound than the desert experience, idolatry, and heresy represent; it is a liberation from the slavery of sin. The word "sin" means everything from which man and mankind must be rescued. It describes the sharpest opposition to God and his salvation.

Who is to be freed from this slavery is indicated by the rather ambiguous expression: "his people." The Jew knew only one people that rightly bore this name in the deepest sense, and that people was Israel, the chosen people. He would say "our people," or would expect from an angel "your people," the people through which alone the Israelite was what he was. Or one might have

expected " the people of God." But here we have, " his people."
From the first moment, this child is accorded a people of his
own, and it is left entirely open whether or not this people is
identical with the present Israel. There could also be question
of a new people, for which present boundaries are no longer
valid, which extends beyond the frontiers of Israel—a new people
of God, which belongs in a special way to Jesus, which bears his
name.

*[22]All this took place to fulfill what the Lord spoke through the
prophet who said: [23]" Behold, the virgin shall conceive and bear
a son, and they shall call him by the name of Emmanuel, which
means, ' God with us '."*

What the angel has declared up to this point is important and
breathtaking. Part of what he says tells clearly what will happen,
the rest hints at far-reaching consequences which the well-in-
formed like Joseph know or at least suspect. St. Matthew ends
the passage with a reference to the fulfillment of a prophecy.
Now it is perfectly clear that this is no everyday event. The
event is full of meaning for the present in which the miracle of
the Holy Spirit takes place, for the future in which this child
will accomplish the salvation of his people, and for the past which
appears in a new light. In a situation full of menace the prophet
Isaiah had announced to King Achaz a divine sign which was to
portend disaster for him. Now this word becomes a message of
joy: " Behold, the virgin shall conceive . . ." The mysterious
circumstances which had filled Joseph with dismay are not so
disturbingly new. The prophet had already suggested them when
he spoke of a " virgin " who was to bear a son. The virgin birth
wrought by the Spirit was already intimated in the Old Testament. The eyes of faith recognize the action of God through the

centuries and know how to understand the promises of the prophet in the light of their fulfillment.

There is something else in the prophecy: a name which is just as profound and rich as the name " Jesus ": " God with us " (Is. 7:10–16). The knowledge that Yahweh was always with his people was something deeply ingrained in the faith of Israel. It was Israel's distinction and its glory. As it was in the past, so will it also be in the future which the prophets proclaim: " Fear not, for I redeem you; I call you by thy name, you are mine! When you go through the waters, I am with you; and when you go through rivers, they shall not submerge you. When you pass through fire, you shall not be burned and the flames shall not scorch you" (Is. 43:1f.). God was always with his people— in the wars of the patriarchs, in the assemblies at the cultic shrines in the time of the judges, and then especially on the sacred hill of Sion and in the temple, at the anointing of its kings and at the mission of its prophets, in his faithfulness and the bestowal of his salvation, and also as they were scattered among the nations in the captivity. During the years of captivity there remained the lively hope that God would be with his people in the future. It was a fact, and yet it was still but a promise. They could experience the presence of God—and still they had to wait for it. The manner of God's future presence to his people, which remained to be realized, was clearly to be something quite new.

And now it seems to have become reality. The child who is to be born bears the name which is the full description of this hope: " God with us." The nearness of God given here is, therefore, not to be made manifest in any thing or place, but in a man whose nature it is to be God with us. In him and through him God is near and present, more closely and more really than ever before.

²⁴Awakened from his sleep, Joseph did as the angel of the Lord had commanded him, and took Mary to himself. ²⁵And he knew her not until she gave birth to her son. And he called his name Jesus.

Joseph does as he was told—simply and unquestioningly. Full of awe and reverence, he refrains from approaching Mary, who now takes her place in the eyes of all as his wedded wife. She gives birth to the child and Joseph designates it by the name " Jesus." Thus it is legally his child, incorporated into the line of ancestors which stretches back to David. We now have knowledge not only of the name which the child is to bear (and which along with the title of Messiah grew into the double name of Jesus Christ, that is, Jesus the Messiah).

The Homage of the Magi (2:1–12)

¹When Jesus was born in Bethlehem of Judea in the days of King Herod, behold, wise men from the East arrived in Jerusalem ²asking, " Where is the newly born king of the Jews? For we have seen his star in the East and have come to pay him homage."

The genealogy and the story of the birth of Jesus remain in the circle of the Jewish land and people. Now the field of view widens to take in the great world of nations and kingdoms. Matthew has already pointed to some of the prophecies which were fulfilled. The episode of the Magi points to the fulfillment of another great text of prophecy—with this difference, that here something occurs in far greater publicity, something that hitherto could only be recognized by the eyes of faith, that is, the advent of the true Messiah.

For the first time we learn in Matthew that the birth of Jesus took place in Bethlehem, in the land of Juda. Both fulfill the prophecy according to which there can be question only of the royal land of Juda, and of a city lying in this land. The two place-names in verse 1 already anticipate the Old Testament quotation which is given in full in verse 6. The prophet Micah had made the assertion about this little town, saying that out of it the ruler of the last days would go forth, the ruler who was to reign over the whole people of Israel. Thus the place of birth is designated by the prophet just as the name of the child was fixed by God.

The text speaks in general of " the days of King Herod," without giving us any closer indication of the date. Herod " the Great " is meant, who, in spite of considerable achievements, carried on a reign of terror and despotism; a foreigner (an Idumaean), and dependent on the goodwill of Rome, he was unscrupulous and licentious. To be sure, he had restored the temple magnificently and conferred many benefits on the people. Nonetheless, the pious circles of the Jews looked on him as a foreign master. Though his power was small, he used the title " king " granted him by Rome. This title is used several times here in contrast to the king whom the Magi are seeking. Jesus is spoken of as " King of the Jews " only twice in the gospel : here in contrast to the despot Herod, and again towards the end, during his trial, when he is so called by the heathen Pilate (27 : 11), by the soldiers as they mock him (27 : 29), and in the inscription on the cross (27 : 32). Jesus indeed says " yes " to Pilate's question (27 : 11), but the title is no expression for the true dignity of Jesus and did not become an element of the profession of faith. Here we are to imagine the ostensible king of the Jews trembling on his throne— while the true king comes in the weakness of a child.

The Magi come from the East. Their homeland is not indicated and their number is not given. External circumstances are passed over in face of the one question which moves them: " Where is the new-born King of the Jews?" They are learned men, probably Babylonian priests familiar with the course of the stars and their rising. A remarkable phenomenon in the stars started them on their journey. They call it " his star," the star of the new child-king. According to the beliefs of the ancient East, the movements of the stars and the destiny of men were intrinsically connected. To this day, however, all the acute research and study which have been made about this star, whether it means a certain constellation, a comet, or a wholly miraculous phenomenon, have led to no clear conclusion. This much is certain: the God of the nations and of the universe sends a sign. The chief thing is not the outward circumstances of the phenomenon but its intrinsic end and object.

But what does the sign mean to the learned men? In their eyes the land of the Jews is ridiculously small and politically insignificant; for centuries it had been incapable of playing an independent role within the Near East. Why is an inquiry made through envoys not enough? Why are they anxious to go there themselves to pay homage? Scripture gives no answer to these questions but only recounts what happened.

God not only led his people out of the Egyptian captivity but he also chose for himself a holy city (Jerusalem) and a holy mountain (Sion). Israel awaited as the dawn of salvation not only the coming of the Messiah and the restoration of the royal rule of David, but much more—the blessing of all the nations through Israel. City and mountain are the place and origin of the salvation which is to be bestowed on the nations. There the light rises; there must men pay homage. At the end of days many nations set out from the four quarters of the world and go on pilgrimage to Jerusalem so that God may teach them his ways and that they may walk in his paths (see Is. 2:2f.). Kings and princes come from all over the earth to bring their gifts into the city of Jerusalem which is bright with glorious light (see Is. 60:3–6; Ps. 72:10f.). The pilgrimage of the nations at the end of time: perhaps this is the picture which the evangelist has before his eyes.

But it is not in the royal city of David that Jesus comes into the world, but in the far more insignificant little town of Bethlehem. And how is it that the Messiah is not born in the royal palace of Herod? All that too is attested by the scriptures. In the prophet Micah, Bethlehem is specifically named and honored. It is indeed insignificant and tiny, yet it is great because from it will proceed the ruler of Israel. St. Matthew has rendered the text of the prophet Micah rather freely. Originally it read: " And you, Bethlehem of Ephrata, small indeed among the towns of Juda, from you shall go forth for me one who is to be ruler over Israel. And his going forth is from of old, since the ages of eternity. Then shall he stand and hold sway, in the might of the Lord, in the majesty of the name of the Lord, his God, and they shall dwell secure, for now his power shall extend to the ends of the earth. And this will be salvation " (Mic. 5:2.4f.). Ephrata was a small clan of Israel, but the one from which David came (1 Sam. 17:11). God had once chosen the weak and in the fullness of days he will do so again.

³When King Herod heard this he was deeply disturbed, and so was all Jerusalem. ⁴And he gathered all the high priests and scribes of the people, and inquired of them where the Messiah was to be born. ⁵They said to him: " In Bethlehem in Judea. For so it is written by the prophet: ⁶"And thou, Bethlehem, land of Judah, thou art far from the least among the princes of Judah. For out

of thee shall go forth a prince, who shall rule my people Israel '."
⁷*Then Herod summoned the Magi secretly and learned exactly*
from them the time that the star had appeared. ⁸*And he sent them*
to Bethlehem saying, " Go and make exact inquiries after the
child. When you have found him, give me word so that I too may
come and pay him homage."

As though to scorn him, Herod is asked about the place. The
question shatters him because he must now fear a new rival and
it dismays the city because it must now tremble at new measures
of terrorism. Since he does not know the place (What does the
king, a friend of pagans and a stranger by blood, know about
the scriptures?), he has to call upon fit counsel—high priests and
scribes who give him an official answer. The place has therefore
not been invented by the belief of Christians nor justified after
the event. The Jews and Herod himself must testify to Bethlehem
as the city of the Messiah!

It is God's own doing that the pilgrimage of the Magi is ter-
minated not in Jerusalem but beyond the city in nearby Bethlehem. A strange and remarkable plan. Jerusalem is not the city of
light where justice and salvation lie ready for the nations. Jerusalem is in the wrong; it is the city of the murderers of the prophets
(23 : 37–39), the city of disobedience and rebellion, of contempt for
the will of God. The Messiah does not come to Jerusalem except
to die there. Then, indeed, light goes forth from this city, but
in a completely different manner than had been expected.

⁹*They, when they had heard the King, went their way. And*
behold, the star that they had seen in the East went before them,
until it came and stopped above the place where the child was.
¹⁰*When they saw the star, they rejoiced with exceedingly great*

joy. ¹¹And entering the house, they saw the child with Mary his mother, and they bowed down and adored him, and opening their treasures they offered him gifts: gold and frankincense and myrrh. ¹² And being warned in a dream not to turn back to Herod, they retired by another way into their own country.

In the midst of poverty and want, something of the great promise is realized in Bethlehem. The learned men find the child and Mary his mother. They offer their homage and precious gifts, such as are due to kings: gold, frankincense, and myrrh. Their joy surpasses all bounds: " They rejoiced with exceedingly great joy." It is the joy of discovery, of longings fulfilled.

It is a beginning, the first part of the homage of all nations to the one Lord. The light is not there only for the Jews. The ruler will not only " rule my people Israel " (v. 6), the heathens, too, have a share in him; indeed, they first of all, before a single Jew has come to the faith. While Herod hardens in grim thoughts of murder, these heathens from the East kneel down before the child. But Herod's plan fails. His hypocritical intention of coming also to pay homage is thwarted: with a gentle hand God gives the Magi directions to return home by another route.

The Flight into Egypt

¹³When they had departed, behold, an angel of the Lord appeared to Joseph in a dream and said: " Rise up, take the child and his mother and flee into Egypt, and stay there till I tell you. For Herod is going to seek out the child, to kill him." ¹⁴So he rose up and took the child and his mother by night and fled into Egypt.

A theme that was announced in the story of the Magi is now

developed further: the attempt of Herod on the life of the child. Tradition says that the child was brought to Egypt by divine intervention. Once more it is Joseph who stands in the foreground. For the second time he receives a message from God, which is brought by an angel. As briefly as before (1:20), the directions are given: " Rise up!" Something is suddenly demanded of him. In the middle of the night he must rouse himself. The intimation is given under cover of sleep, when the higher levels of consciousness are obscured, but its execution calls for decisive action. Hence Joseph gets up and acts without delay.

" He took the child and his mother." In the first two chapters of the gospel Mary and the child Jesus are spoken of only in these terms (2:11,13,14,20,21). First comes the child, who is always placed at the central point, and only then comes Mary who bore him. St. Matthew never says: " his parents " or " the family " or " Mary and her child." The two sacred persons are kept distinct, corresponding to the difference in their dignity.

Mary is not designated by her name, but only as " his mother." This does not mean that she is kept coldly at a distance, but that she receives her dignity from the child. Her name is mentioned only once in the first two chapters (1:18), while the proper name " Joseph " is constantly used. Her glory rests on her election to be the true and real human mother of the Messiah.

" And flee into Egypt." There had already been an emigration to Egypt when famine drove the children of Jacob into the fertile delta of the Nile (Gen. 42f.). Necessity commanded there, too: flight from death by starvation. Egypt had been from ancient times the refuge in time of need for all the surrounding lands. The desert tribes especially were often driven to the borders of the cultivated land in order to keep themselves alive. The way to the south was difficult and not without danger, but it was near at

hand. Only a few days' journey was necessary to reach the borders
of the rich delta. Now Joseph is to take the same way to save the
life of the child who has been entrusted to him. God prepares
a refuge for us at the right time without our having to be anxious
beforehand. Even in the final tribulations which are described in
the Book of Revelation God has made a refuge in the desert for
the community of the end of days to enable them to escape the
greatest and fiercest assault of evil (Rev. 12:6). What he has
granted to his Son, he will not refuse to the brothers of his Son.

"And stay there till I tell you." The angel leaves Joseph
uncertain. Thus he is obliged to do only that which he was
ordered. Here, too, his openness for the inspiration from God
must prove itself again. The will of God must be done, not
only as we perceive it in secret intimations or in the many occasions of daily life, but also when it comes as the exigent will of
God. A man must be very well practiced indeed in living with
this will to be prepared for such a command as Joseph here
receives.

But the angel also adds an explanation for the command. "For
Herod is going to seek out the child to kill him." The grave
word, which actually means "destroy," "annihilate," "do away
with by force," has a terrible ring at this point. Later on, Jesus
will say of the wicked husbandmen who have put the son to death
that the Lord of the vineyard will annihilate them (21:41). The
contrast could not be sharper. Here heathens with believing hearts
hasten to pay their homage; there the King of the Jews plotted
to put the child-king to death.

15*And he stayed there until the death of Herod so that the
prophecy might be fulfilled which the Lord had spoken through
the prophet who said: "Out of Egypt have I called my son."*

With the death of Herod the darkness seems to lift somewhat. For Joseph was there " until the death of Herod."

The evangelist rounds off the passage with a fulfillment quotation from the prophet Hosea. This stay abroad is also willed by God. Boldly and yet profoundly, the writer sees the prophecy fulfilled: " Out of Egypt have I called my son." The prophet said that of Israel as a whole, which, while it was still young and a child, had been chosen lovingly by God and called to wander forth: " When Israel was a child, I loved him; out of Egypt I called my son " (Hos. 11 : 1). That was the time of the first bridal love in which Israel was entirely given to his God and knew no idols. So now God calls his real Son out of Egypt back to the land of the fathers. We can hear in the words not only the harmony of a prophecy accomplished; we can see not only the two historical events in their resemblance to one another; but over and beyond, we can feel some of the soaring hopes which filled the soul of Hosea. Like the springtime in the youth of Israel, God will grant, after Israel's conversion, a second spring, a life of undivided dedication to the Lord. " Therefore, behold, I will entice her and lead her out into the wilderness and speak to her heart. And I will give her her vineyards, and change the Valley of Achor into the Gate of Hope. There shall she answer, as in the days of her youth, as in the days when she went up out of the land of Egypt " (Hos. 2 : 14f.; see 12 : 10)

The Massacre of the Innocents in Bethlehem (2:16–18)

[16]*Then Herod, seeing that he had been fooled by the Magi, was furiously angry. And he sent and killed all the male children in*

Bethlehem and in all that region who were two years of age and under, corresponding to the time which he had ascertained from the Magi.

Up to this point, St. Matthew has only spoken of the rescue of the child-Messiah. But even with his escape danger has not been entirely averted. On the contrary, Herod gives savage vent to his anger. He recognizes that the Magi have circumvented him. He is left with his anxiety, and all he has to go on is the date of the appearance of the star which he had learned from the Magi (2:7). His terror is so great and he is so unscrupulous that he orders a massacre. If he cannot locate and identify the child-king, Herod must take measures to see that he does not live. Thus he has all the male children under two years of age put to death.

Once more note the strange parallel to the events in Egypt during the youth of Israel. There it was a Pharaoh who feared the strength and vitality of the Israelites so much that he gave the order for the killing of their sons: " Throw into the Nile all the boys that are born to the Hebrews, but let all the girls live " (Ex. 1:22). Just as at that time the dreadful massacre could not thwart God's plan of preserving the saviour in the person of Moses, so too the child-Messiah is now saved from the massacre in Bethlehem. In this episode too, Matthew tells only what is necessary. He is interested only in tracing the links in the history wrought by God.

17Then was fulfilled the prophecy uttered by the prophet Jeremiah when he said: 18"A voice was heard in Ramah, weeping and great lamentation; Rachel is mourning her children and she will not be comforted because they are no more."

" Rachel is mourning her children." Once more it is a prophetic text which supplies the evangelist with the key (Jer. 31 : 15). He is not embarrassed by the fact that Jeremiah speaks of Ramah, which lies to the north of Jerusalem, and not of Bethlehem, which lies to the south; for the lamentation is the same. There the prophet hears how Rachel, the ancestor of the tribes of Benjamin and Ephraim, weeps for her children who are exiled and captive in Assyria. The land has been stripped of its people, the towns left deserted. The desolation of the land is also in her soul. It was a disaster which disclosed the whole tragedy of Israel, its national misfortune, and its disobedience against God which brought upon it the misfortune. The pain of the mothers in Bethlehem is of the same sort. So the evangelist does not hear merely the lament over the loss of the children. In it can be heard also the sorrow for the disobedience of Israel. For the cruel deed done then was done, after all, in Israel, and by a king of Israel. This massacre is like a signal, a cry of alarm, which reveals the smoldering evil.

The Transfer to Nazareth (2:19–23)

[19]*But when Herod was dead, behold, an angel of the Lord appeared in a dream to Joseph in Egypt* [20]*and said: " Rise up, take the child and his mother and go to the land of Israel. For they who sought the life of the child are dead."* [21]*So he rose up and took the child and his mother and entered the land of Israel.*

Earlier (2 : 15), the death of Herod had already been mentioned, and now the event itself and its effects on the holy family are spoken of again. The occasion of the change of domicile is acci-

dental—the death of the cruel and watchful king. And still such
an extrinsic occasion is able to direct the destiny of the child-
Messiah! Does that not seem to be a weakness on the part of God
to allow his actions to be determined by the moods and destinies
of men? Later in the life of Jesus we find much the same thing.
The occasion for his public ministry also stems from circumstances outside himself, the imprisonment of John the Baptist
(Mk. 1:14). An effort made against him by Herod Antipas causes
Jesus to conceal himself (Lk. 13:31–33). Does God let men prescribe his course of action and take out of his hands the guidance
of events? Such an impression touches only the surface of history.
In the depths, however, all that happens, and happens with inexorable necessity, is what God wills. Matthew leads us to this
depth by the light thrown on events by the revelation of the Old
Testament.

The angel directs Joseph almost in the same words as when
commanding him to flee (2:13) to go into the " land of Israel "
with the child and his mother. The expression has a religious
tinge. The heavenly messenger does not give the political designation of the territories (Judea, Samaria, Galilee), nor any geographical indication such as Palestine. He uses the expression
which describes this land in the Old Testament as the land of
God, the gift of his mercy. It is the " holy land," graciously
bestowed on the twelve tribes of Israel. Here Matthew uses the
expression twice. He means to indicate that Jesus enters the land
of the patriarchs which is bestowed anew on the Messiah. Do we
not also hear the themes of the Exodus from Egypt and the taking possession of Palestine in the " springtime " of the people?
" Out of Egypt have I called my son " (2:15)—" go into the land
of Israel."

That these cross-references, like undertones and overtones, play their part is shown by the reason which the angel adds: " For they who sought the life of the child are dead." This is taken almost word for word from the story of the Exodus where the phrase is addressed to Moses. He had had to flee from Egypt, where, after killing the Egyptian overseer, he was a " wanted man," and had to spend long years in a foreign country, the land of Midian. There he received his mission (Ex. 3:1–8), and at a given moment, the command to go back to accomplish his allotted task. " And the Lord said to Moses in Midian : ' Go and return to Egypt. For they are all dead who sought your life.' And Moses took his wife and his children and put them on an ass and went back to Egypt " (Ex. 4:19). Is this not a strange interplay of the dispositions of Providence? There the Pharaoh who wishes to destroy the youthful Moses; here Herod who seeks to kill the child-Messiah. There the flight *from* Egypt and the return by the order of God; here the flight *into* Egypt and the return by God's command. There the chosen liberator with his wife and sons on the move; here the son of David, Joseph, the instrument of God's guidance, with " the child and his mother," leaving their home. But these subsidiary parallels are, as it were, only the accompaniment to the great parallels which Matthew sees: the exodus out of Egypt, the liberation from bondage, the new people of God. He knows all this now about the child Jesus and indicates it briefly by allusions to the early history of Israel.

²²Hearing, however, that Archelaus was reigning in Judea in the place of his father Herod, he was afraid to go there. And being warned in a dream, he retired into the region of Galilee. When he arrived there he settled in a town called Nazareth. This was to fulfill what was said by the prophets: " He shall be called a Nazarene."

After the death of Herod (4 B.C), the territory was divided into new realms. Galilee in the north went to his son Herod Antipas, Judea and Samaria to his son Herod Archelaus. The latter was even more savage than his father and was soon removed from office by the Roman Emperor (6 A.D.). For the present, however, he was the reigning king. Apparently his evil reputation soon became widely known. Joseph " was afraid " to enter his realm. So he turned north " to the region of Galilee." It does not appear that Joseph makes this move alone; for the hand of God is seen in his decision. Here once more a situation is imposed by political circumstances. That Christ should come from Nazareth is one of the oddest circumstances of his life.

Galilee alone would make him suspect, for this region was looked on as half-heathen, easygoing, earthy, and primitive by the Jews who were zealous for the law. Still more, his origin from Nazareth: " Can anything good come out of Nazareth?" says Nathanael to Philip (Jn. 1:46). It was precisely from this place, and not from one of the more respectable cities around the lake of Genesareth, like Tiberias or Bethsaida, that Jesus started out.

The name " Jesus of Nazareth " must be very ancient, perhaps the earliest way of speaking of Jesus used by his contemporaries. Was it perhaps forged by opponents who wanted to hold him up to derision by this title? It is possible. But the seeming contradiction is enough by itself: Jesus—that is, the Saviour and " God with us "; —Nazareth, that is, the discredited and contemptible place. Can we not feel, in the choice of this particular place, something of God's self-emptying?

When Joseph takes up his abode in Nazareth God's will is again fulfilled thereby. It is contained in the scriptures, obscurely no doubt and apparently not to be found without some artificiality, but recognizable to the instinct of faith: " He shall be called a Nazarene." In this form the saying is given nowhere in the Old Testament. And the indication " by the prophets " does not add anything precise. What was in Matthew's mind? The prophet Isaiah says of the future Messiah: " A shoot shall come forth from the stump of Jesse, and a branch shall flourish from his roots, and the Spirit of the Lord shall rest upon him " (Is. 11:1). From the stump of Jesse, the ancestral tree of David which had been slashed and rendered unfruitful by God's judgment, a new shoot is to spring. " Shoot " in Hebrew is " *nezer,*" which sounds something like " *nozri,*" the " Nazorean," which was perhaps only later given the meaning of " man of Nazareth." The most probable explanation is this relation between " man of Nazareth " and the " shoot from the stump of Jesse." But then this origin is neither contemptible nor suspect. On the contrary, it is a reference to the Messiah and saviour.

THE WORK OF THE MESSIAH IN GALILEE
(3—18)

The Beginnings (3:1—4:22)

John the Baptist (3:1-12)

John the Baptist is in the foreground in the first section of the public ministry of Jesus. First his entry on the scene is described (3:1-6). Then follow two items from his activity as a preacher: his preaching of repentance (3:7-10) and his announcement of the Messiah (3:11-12). The high point of his work is the baptism of Jesus (3:13-17), which is, however, already an introduction to the activity of Jesus.

THE COMING OF THE BAPTIST (3:1-6)

The author passes from the early days of the Messiah's childhood to his coming appearance as a man without giving any connecting links. With seeming carelessness this new section is introduced by the words: "In those days . . ." We are not told the age of Jesus. St. Matthew is always primarily interested not in the historical details or the colorful variety of events, but in their inner meaning, their intention, and what they assert about God and Jesus Christ. The evangelist proclaims them primarily for the faith of his hearers. Everything that we read is primarily the testimony of faith—born of the faith and ordained for our faith.

¹In those days John the Baptist appeared preaching in the desert of Judea ²and said: " Repent! For the kingdom of heaven is at hand."

The first sentence gets right to the point: the message of the Baptist in verse 2. We learn only a few details of this tremendous hour. " John the Baptist appeared." This is the first mention of him, but he is spoken of as a well-known figure. Only his proper name is mentioned, and " the Baptist " added like a fixed surname. Everyone knows who he is; his coming had a profound effect upon his times.

" Preaching in the desert of Judea." His word is the main thing. He proclaimed, he called out, he summoned . . . for the Greek word means the proclamation of a message by a herald. In the desert of Judea: this is the region of grey, unfertile rock which stretches from the upland of Judea down to the Jordan valley and the Dead Sea. The call of the herald comes from outside. He does not enter into the noise and activity in the streets and squares. Like a fanfare he resounds from afar, lonely and unaccompanied. The desert is the place of purity and barrenness. Nothing gets in the way of God and prevents the hearing of his word. The time of the desert wandering is the ideal of the time of salvation: " Like grapes in the desert I once found Israel, like early fruit on the young fig tree I looked upon your fathers " (Hos. 9:10). Salvation will come out of the desert: " Behold, now I create a new thing; it grows already, do you not perceive it? Yes, I am making a way through the wilderness and streams through the desert " (Is. 43:19; see 41:18–20). At the time of Jesus, the Messiah was expected to come out of the desert: " If they say to you, behold, he is in the desert " (Mt. 24:26).

The message is as terse and great as it could possibly be. It contains two phrases. The first is: " Repent!" The prophet is recognized by this call. " Return!", " Be converted "—this was the constantly recurring call handed on like a torch from one prophet to another calling men back to God. This call reaches a climax in Ezekiel where it is bound up with the promise of life. Perfect conversion of thought and life is demanded: " ' Repent and turn away from all your sins. Cast away from you all your sins which you have committed against me, and get yourselves a new heart and a new spirit! Why would you die, O house of Israel? For I desire not the death of anyone who dies,' says the Lord God. Be converted then, and live " (Ez. 18:30–32). The wandering that leads to death should end in life. The sins that burden the heart must be cast away, and instead, a new heart fully given to God and a new spirit animating and impelling this heart must be procured. The call of the Baptist is to be understood in this wide sense. It is a matter of life or death, destruction or salvation. Then as ever.

Never before had a prophet based this call on such a reason: " For the kingdom of heaven is at hand." The prophets used the threat of the judgment of God, the eruption of his anger, the infliction of penalties, the dreadful " Day of the Lord ": " The Day of the Lord shall be darkness, not light, somber and without brightness " (Amos 5:20). A man like Amos feels the urgent force and the oppressive nearness of this day. Its imminence gives his call to repentance an overwhelming might. Is the event under whose shadow the Baptist stands this dark day on which the anger of God is to unleash its flames on Israel and the nations? The answer must be yes if one listens to his preaching of repentance (3:7–10). But here, at the beginning, where he uses the expression " kingdom of heaven," this is impossible. The phrase has a bright tone of joyful hope. It means the establishment of God's kingly rule over all the world and for all time, God's brilliant triumph at the end of history, the bliss and joy of all who belong to God.

It is remarkable that the first words which Jesus proclaims, according to the account in Matthew, are exactly the same (4 : 17). Did the Baptist proclaim nothing different from Jesus? As precursor and path-finder, should he not be more reserved and speak only of repentance and conversion? Should he not leave the announcement of the great joy to him who comes after him? That is certainly true and the passages which follow demonstrate it clearly. But St. Matthew wants to tell us that John the Baptist already forms part of the new age; with him the kingdom of God already begins to become reality. And thereby something else, too, is said: No matter how stern is his preaching of repentance, and no matter how much it is dominated by the terrors of the " Day of the Lord," it is finally in the service of the glad event, the joyous message, the rising light of salvation. His word is not meant to weigh men down, but to lift them up. He demands a strict conversion, but for the sake of a glorious object, and that is the greatest that we know and can imagine, the kingship of God.

³" *For this is he who is spoken of by the prophet Isaiah, when he said: ' The voice of one who calls out in the wilderness, Prepare the way of the Lord, make straight his paths '.*"

Once more it is significant that we hear first of his place in the plan of God and only then of the details of his entry on the scene. Isaiah had described his office beforehand, when he cried out to the weary exiles in Babylon: " Hark, a voice cries: ' In the wilderness prepare the way of the Lord; make in the desert a straight path for our God. Every valley shall fill up, and every mountain and hill shall sink down, the crags shall become a plain, and the heights level ground. And the glory of the Lord shall be revealed, and all flesh shall see it together; for the mouth of the Lord has spoken ' " (Is. 40:3–5). The prophet saw a splendid procession making its way through the desert to the fatherland (Is. 40:9–11). With great daring the church and the evangelist hear this word in a new way and understand it of John. He it is who called and still calls: " Prepare the way of the Lord." Isaiah could not say who uttered the cry, but we know. God was to make his entry along with the people in this triumphal procession, but now there comes in person he who bears the name " God with us." From the whole picture the eyes of faith can grasp the two figures: the messenger and herald is John, and the " Lord " is the Messiah. Redemption from bondage draws nigh.

⁴But he, John, wore a garment of camel's hair, and a leather girdle round his waist, and his food was locusts and wild honey. ⁵Then Jerusalem streamed out to him and all Judea and the whole region of Jordan.

The Baptist's way of life is austere; his life testifies to what he demands of others.

The call does not go unheeded. A great pilgrimage gets under way. But it is not the pilgrimage which the prophet foresaw, that is, the liberated people *en route* to its homeland. Here they travel into the desert, to the man of God, not to seek a sensation, but to renew their lives. The expressions may be exaggerated, but it is certain that something profoundly frightened the people of Juda to their feet and drove them out to John.

⁶And they were baptized by him in the river Jordan, confessing their sins.

All who came out to him were baptized by him. This practice became so distinctive of him that he received the surname of " the Baptist." In the Jordan, probably not far from where it flows into the Dead Sea, he performed the rite of immersion with each individual. Their sins were to be symbolically washed away. It is true that in his day ablutions and baths were in use among the official circles of Judaism, as in certain communities or sects. But these rites were part of the daily, standard elements of life according to the law. The baptism of John is something done once for all, a sign of conversion, of the renewal of man, of readiness for the approaching salvation : " Wash yourselves, purify yourselves! Get rid of your evil deeds, take them out of my sight! Cease to do evil, learn to do good " (Is. 1 : 16f.). Whoever was immersed in the river in this way should live henceforward as a new man, his whole heart set on what is to come.

The Preaching of Repentance (3 : 7–10)

7*When he saw many of the Pharisees and Sadducees coming to the baptism, he said to them: " You brood of vipers! Who has taught you that you could flee from the wrath [of judgment] to come? 8Bring therefore fruit which befits repentance!"*

Among the pilgrims were not only simple people, but also merchants and soldiers, pious Pharisees and members of the council from Jerusalem. It is worth noting that the only detailed piece of his preaching which the evangelist records is directed specifically to that group. St. Matthew undoubtedly means that the sharp address, " brood of vipers," fits those precisely who reveal themselves as such in the course of the gospel (see 12 : 34; 23 : 33). But there can be no doubt that this passage contains the basic thought of the Baptist's preaching. It explains the first programmatic word: " Do penance!"

" Who has taught you that you could flee from the wrath [of judgment] to come?" The day of catastrophe and destruction, the day of Yahweh, stands before the gate; it " draws on " with such might and swiftness that none can escape it: " It shall be as though one fled from a lion and a bear came upon him, or came into his house and leaned his hand upon the wall, and a snake bit him " (Amos 5 : 19). Whoever thinks himself secure will be all the more surely seized. Whoever seeks a refuge, will find his hiding place a trap. This day breaks in upon you, too, it leaves no one a way of escape. " For great is the Day of the Lord and terrible; who can endure it?" (Joel 2 : 11).

There is, however, a " flight," a way which does not preserve one from the Day itself but helps one to survive it. The Day comes, but not as judgment and wrath, if you are converted: " Bring therefore fruit which befits repentance." Penitence is the one thing that can save you: leave the path which leads to death for that which leads to life; cast out sin and choose God. Repentance must prove itself in deeds. A new way of thinking, a change of mind and spirit is not enough; the whole life must be changed.

[9]" And do not believe that you can say to yourselves: ' We have Abraham for our father.' For I tell you that God can raise up children to Abraham from these stones. [10]The axe is already laid to the roots of the trees. And now every tree that does not yield good fruit shall be cut down and cast into the fire."

But how is it with our certainties, with our guarantees? Are we not the chosen people, endowed with promises and privileges in all abundance? Are we not children of Abraham, " the father," and by our common descent sharers of the promise made to him? Will not his " merits " be imputed to us so that we need not fear for our salvation? But John says: " Do not believe you can say to yourselves because we have Abraham for our father. For I tell you: God can raise up children to Abraham from these stones!" That is unheard-of, it is heresy! God pays no attention to the privileges? Look at the red stones lying about. God is not short of children, of true sons. If it is not you, since you refuse to do penance, then God creates a new race for Abraham out of these stones. That must have stirred everybody, and shocked and upset the self-assured, orthodox Jews who were well-versed in scripture. Certainly, God has set up an order of salvation; certainly, he stands by his promise, even to the chosen people. But no one can use this to obtain automatically forgiveness, salvation, and life. That each one must accomplish himself, even in the church, even today.

One already has a feeling that the old frame of things is being shattered and that another Israel is coming on the horizon, one which does not coincide with the national community of Judaism. St. Paul will call Abraham the " father of all uncircumcised believers," and also the " father of the circumcised," but only of such as imitate him in faith (Rom. 4:11f.). John intends to shake the security only of those who are just in their own eyes; he cannot yet have thought of an Israel " from among the heathens." But the paths have already been pointed out and St. Paul is the first to go along them. What an upheaval is announced here! This is truly the " preparation of a way," the " straightening of the paths."

Time is short and there can be no delay, not even for repen-

tance: " The axe is already being laid to the roots of the trees."
A few more blows and the trees will crack and fall. You must
hurry, delay not a moment longer! Now the metaphors penetrate one another: the trees, the fruit of the trees, the axe to cut
them down. If the axe is swung, it surely strikes, just as none can
escape the day of wrath. When one is converted, his tree is indeed
felled but it is not burned. It can survive in the fire of destruction.
All others are vowed to destruction: every tree that does not
bring forth good fruit is cut down and cast into the fire. The fire
is the fire of destructive judgment. All that have not been converted will be devoured by it.

The Announcement of the Messiah (3:11–12)

[11]" *I baptize you with water unto repentance; but he who comes*
after me is stronger than I, whose shoes I am not worthy to carry;
he shall baptize you with the Holy Spirit and with fire."

John announces not only the coming of the " Day of the Lord,"
but the closeness of a person. It is given to him to utter what no
prophet dared say before him: " but he who comes after me is
stronger than I." His name is not mentioned, it is simply " he
who comes."

John demonstrates in two images that this other is mightier
than he. The first image speaks of baptism. John's own took place
" in water, for repentance." It was meant for repentance and gave
expression to it. That the baptized had water poured over them
was a summons to the new life which they were to lead. What
John contributed was an external seal and confirmation of this
will, the outward sign of something which the individual had

to accomplish within. But now the stronger comes, who will also perform a baptism, but of an entirely different nature. " He shall baptize you with the Holy Spirit and with fire." Firstly: no longer with water, which rinses only the surface but with the living Spirit of God who changes the heart. What the Spirit of God takes hold of will infallibly be turned into a new creation. This gift is within the power of the stronger one to give.

God's Holy Spirit is a gift of the last days. Isaiah sees the land ravaged and denuded, " till the Spirit from on high is poured out upon us. Then the wilderness will become a fruitful field " (Is. 32:15). He hears God declare: " I will pour out my Spirit upon your children and my blessing upon your offspring " (Is. 44:3). Among the events of the end the prophet Joel includes the outpouring of the Spirit, a prediction which St. Peter sees fulfilled at Pentecost: " And it shall come to pass after this, that I shall pour out my Spirit upon all flesh. And your sons and daughters will prophesy, your old men shall dream dreams, your young men shall see visions. And on your menservants, too, and on your maidservants, I will pour out my Spirit in those days " (Joel 2:28f.).

Secondly: he will also baptize with fire. John had just spoken of the fire of a judgment which was to decree destruction (3:10). That too is an ancient image for the Day of the Lord: " For behold, the day is coming burning like a furnace when all the proud and all that act godlessly shall be like stubble. And the Day that then comes shall set them on fire, says the Lord of Hosts, so that neither root nor branch of them survives " (Mal. 4:1; see Joel 2:1–5). Upon the unconverted the flames close in, on the converted the Spirit is poured out. This is the double baptism. But the first remains in the foreground, as the following verse shows.

[12]*" His winnowing shovel is in his hand, and he will cleanse his threshing floor. He will bring his wheat into his barn, but burn the chaff in unquenchable fire."*

The second picture comes from the life of the husbandman. The grain is gathered in and winnowed on the threshing floor. The chaff is separated from the wheat: the chaff is carried away by the wind, and the heavier grain falls to the floor. The former is burnt, the latter laid up in the barn. This is what is now about to happen. The stronger has already seized the shovel. There remain only a few moments more until the separation begins. But is that not God's own business, his privilege—the passing of judgment? John knows of one judgment only, the judgment of God. When he speaks of it, he has to say everything that the prophets before him had made known about it. But he who exercises it is not God; it is " the stronger one," none other than the Messiah. The picture of the Messiah receives even here, at the beginning, dimensions such as no Jew would have imagined: Lord and judge of the last days. Truly, he is someone " stronger," before whom John himself falls prostrate, feeling himself unqualified even for the humblest task of a slave, namely, carrying the sandals after his Lord. He who was sent to go " before him," feels himself unequal to running " after him " as his servant.

Only a few sentences are written by St. Matthew about the coming and the preaching of the Baptist. But these few sentences give a magnificent picture of the man whom Jesus himself described as the " greatest of those born of woman " (11:11). If he stands so high above all others, and if he then sees the distance between himself and the Messiah as so immense, what then shall we say when *we* are compared to the Messiah?

The Baptism of Jesus (3:13–17)

¹³*Then Jesus came from Galilee to the Jordan and went to John to be baptized by him.* ¹⁴*But John refused, saying, " It is I who need to be baptized by you, and do you come to me?"* ¹⁵*Jesus answered and said to him: " Let it be so now; for thus it is fitting for us to fulfill all justice." So John agreed.*

Jesus comes as one among many and with the intention, expressed in so many words, of being baptized. This had not been said so clearly even of the Pharisees and Sadducees (3:7). That is somewhat strange and the question at once arises: How can one who has just been designated as "the stronger," one to whom such powers have been attributed, now bow down among the weak? Why does he who is to confer baptism with the Holy Spirit cause himself to be washed with water? The other gospels bypass the difficulty and give no answer. In Matthew, the Baptist and Jesus give the answer as soon as they meet.

John must have recognized Jesus at once. With his shocked question, he tries to restrain him from carrying out his intention: " It is I who need to be baptized by you, and do you come to me?" John has not yet been baptized with the baptism of the Spirit which he has just proclaimed and for which he longs. This baptism is described once more as the higher one which is to replace his own, and therefore to divide the old age from the new. The figure of John bridges the dividing line. It is indeed true that none greater than he has arisen among those born of woman, but it is also true that " the least in the kingdom of heaven is greater than he " (Mt. 11:11). His question is not primarily a sign of his personal humility or of his own longing for salvation, but rather the consequence of his preaching: now comes the time of the

" stronger "; he who baptizes in the Spirit and fire can have nothing to do with my baptism of repentance.

Jesus answers him: " Let it be so now." Do not resist, but let what is necessary take its course. " For so it is fitting for us to fulfill all justice." It is extraordinary that Jesus associates himself with the Baptist, and speaks of " us." They who are so unequal in rank that John does not feel himself capable of doing the service of a slave are still side by side in one regard : a charge has now been laid on both of us, which we may not evade. " All justice " is at stake. What God now wants, we must perform obediently in all things. Both of us are under a higher command. The Messiah follows the same path, which in obedience will lead him to death: explaining, therefore, at the very beginning for the sake of all that come after, what is that " justice " which is to surpass by far that of the Pharisees and scribes (see 5 : 20): the suppression of one's own will, a deep inner union with the will of God.

[16]*When Jesus was baptized, he came up immediately out of the water. And behold, the heavens were opened, and he saw the Spirit of God descending like a dove and alighting upon him.* [17]*And behold, a voice spoke from heaven: " This is my beloved Son, in whom I am well pleased."*

This event appears almost as a response to the saying about " all justice." Matthew describes it as a personal experience of the Lord; the public seem to remark nothing. It is something that takes place between himself and the Father, a mystery within the sphere of the divine. Once more we hear of " the Spirit of God." He was already at work in the miraculous conception in the womb of the virgin (1 : 18.20). The beginning of Jesus' life was

the work of the Spirit; the start of his labors is also the work of
the Spirit. When the Spirit descends " upon him," he takes possession of him. This was said of the men of God in the Old
Testament, and above all, it was proclaimed by Isaiah about the
Messiah: " The Spirit of God the Lord rests upon me, because
the Lord has anointed me; he has sent me to bring good tidings
to the poor " (Is. 61 : 1). Every mission has its origin in God
the Lord, but its execution is sustained and impelled by his Holy
Spirit. So too with the Messiah.

To the wordless sign of the descending Spirit is added the voice
of the Father which resounds from heaven : " This is my beloved
Son, in whom I am well pleased." God acknowledges this man
as his own, a man who stands like one of the common people on
the bank of the Jordan, unnoticed and with nothing to distinguish
him. He calls him his " beloved Son." The adjective has indeed
the meaning of " the unique, the only," but in it there is also a
note of warmth and close union in love which we now perceive
for the first time. The Old Testament too speaks of " sons of
God "; the kings of Israel above all receive this title. They stand
particularly close to God, since through them his lordship and his
majesty are mirrored on earth. But never before was anyone
named " my beloved Son " by God himself.

The Father describes Jesus as his Son, not to present him to the
world, or to reveal himself personally to him, but to acknowledge
him as his own. " In him I am well pleased " indicates that the
work that will soon begin bears expressly and from the very start
the seal of divine approbation. This is what God will mean by
raising the crucified from the dead and he bears witness to it
already at the very beginning. Beginning and end correspond to
one another like two pillars on which the bridge rests.

The Temptation in the Desert (4:1–11)

¹*Then Jesus was led out into the desert by the Spirit, to be tempted by the devil.* ²*When he had fasted for forty days and forty nights, he was hungry.* ³*And the tempter approached him and said to him: " If you are the Son of God, command that these stones become loaves of bread." ⁴But he answered: " It is written: ' Not by bread alone does man live, but by every word that comes from the mouth of God '."*

Full of the Spirit, Jesus stands by the Jordan. We see at once how the mighty force works within him: " The Spirit led him into the desert." John had already lived there; now Jesus also is directed there. So what now follows is also willed by God. It is strange how the ways of God seem to be determined by a law : salvation comes out of the desert. It is the place of pure worship of God, as the people wandered through the desert, as they returned from the captivity in Babylon, as John, as Jesus practiced it. Here the desert becomes the place of decision for or against God. A decision which is not brought in for the sake of clarifying his personal mission, but for or against the salvation of all men and of the world. So the first sentence hastens to give the object of his stay in the desert: " to be tempted by the devil."

The history of Israel from beginning to end shows that there existed mighty forces which constantly worked against the establishment of the kingship of God, forces which manifested themselves in crude violence or in the disguise of refinement, using as their outward instrument mighty states or the weakness of individual men. The forms are myriad, but the object is always the same: God must not be Lord, his will shall not prevail, his plan may not be realized. Only in the last centuries before Christ does Israel see things more clearly, and behind all the manifold forms a personal force is discerned. Now, at the very first moment that the work of God is to be done, the adversary is also on the spot. Here it is not a matter of human, everyday temptations; God and Satan meet in undisguised and inflexible opposition to one another.

Jesus had fasted forty days and forty nights in the desert as Moses had done before him on Mount Sinai (Ex. 34:28). When he is in a state of sharp hunger and bodily exhaustion the evil one approaches him with the challenge to make bread out of stones. Clearly, something easy for the Son of God, and at the same time sensible. Isn't this a minor temptation of little importance?

Jesus rejects it with a saying of scripture which is taken from Deuteronomy. When Moses addresses the people he reminds them that God has marvelously sustained them in the desert in spite of hardship and hunger (Deut. 8:3). For the fathers in the desert that was an important experience. God had preserved their lives in a marvelous way. But they had to believe Moses and so trust in God. Must it not be the same for the Messiah? He is not to rely on his own power but to place all his trust in God. Since God has led him into the desert, will he not preserve his life? In this way, too, Jesus fulfills " all justice "—and becomes the perfect example for all that will imitate him : God takes care of his own as soon as they look to him. His all-powerful word could of course make bread of stones. But he rewards the confidence of the Messiah much more providentially : angels come to wait on him (4:11).

5Then the devil took him into the holy city, and placed him on the pinnacle of the temple, 6and said to him: " If you are the Son of God, cast yourself down. For it is written: ' He will give his angels charge over you, and with their hands they will lift you up, lest you dash your foot against a stone '." ⁷Jesus said to him: " It is written also: ' Thou shalt not tempt the Lord thy God '."

The second temptation brings him " into the holy city." This is Jerusalem, to which St. Matthew alone gives this reverent title. The two of them are standing on the pinnacle of the temple roof. The devil challenges him to throw himself down headlong, trusting in the word of the psalm, according to which God will charge his angels to see that no harm comes to the pious whom he loves (Ps. 91:11f.). How much more will this promise hold good for the " Son of God "! In the first temptation Jesus' confidence in God had proved itself admirably. All the same, it should not be difficult to put the confidence just expressed to the proof once more. Prove what you have just confessed by a courageous deed. If this confidence is so mighty and total, my proposition cannot be looked on as excessive.

Since the tempter is well versed in scripture, Jesus answers him likewise with a saying from scripture which breaks through the fine spun web of his opponent: " Thou shalt not tempt the Lord, thy God " (Deut. 6:16). If I did what you suggest, says Jesus, I would not be giving a proof of my confidence but rather the opposite: " *peirasmos,*" temptation, the great temptation to apostasy and estrangement. God does not permit anyone to prescribe what help he should give and he will not be made the servant of man. His intervention is always the free gift of grace, even for the Messiah. His confidence is of course unlimited, but unlimited precisely in the sense that he can do nothing of himself, but only what he sees the Father doing (Jn. 5:19). God must be absolute sovereign and in all things.

[8]Then the devil took him to a mountain of enormous height, and showed him all the kingdoms of the world and their glory [9]and said to him: " All these will I give you, if you bow down and pay me homage." [10]And Jesus said to him: " Begone, Satan! For it is written: ' To the Lord your God shall you pay homage, and him only shall you worship '." [11]At that the devil let him go, and behold, angels came and waited on him.

Here at last the evil one uses clear language. Things have come finally to a head, and though Jesus answers once more with a quotation from scripture, his own personal word of command is also given : " Begone, Satan!" It is already made clear that the higher power dwells in him, and that he can even rule over someone who believes that possession of the world is vested in him. A clear and direct word of command is enough to drive Satan from the field. Jesus gives it apparently in his own name out of the fullness of his own powers, and yet he says in the same breath : " To the Lord your God shall you pay homage, and him only shall you worship." He has the power, but it is not his own. He drives off the tempter, but not in his own name. Here and precisely here God alone is in view. He is the only one who can demand homage and worship.

" And behold, angels came and waited on him." What a remarkable change of scenery. Jesus has just refused to make any effort to gain power; he has proclaimed his confidence in God; and he has put himself entirely at the disposition of his Father— now he himself receives the ready and willing service of heavenly beings. Just as in the earlier account of the baptism, so is it here. First he empties himself to fulfill obediently all justice, and then God acknowledges him as his beloved Son. Here again he accepts

God's lordship without reserve and then God sends him the heavenly envoys to serve him.

There is a phrase in the passage which takes us still deeper into the meaning of the strange episode. Satan promises " all the kingdoms of the world and their glory." In Jesus' preaching we shall be constantly meeting the phrase " kingdom of God," or, as it is nearly always called in Matthew, the " kingdom of heaven." This always means the assertion and establishment of the lordship of God, his royal rule. It is Jesus' deepest interest and the center of his mission. What the adversary says is already an indication of this. Clearly, he knows that what is at stake is not only Jesus as a person, his messianic mission, his sonship of God (4:3.6), but something still greater: the kingly sovereignty of God. Using the same notion of " kingdom," he tries to capture Jesus and impress him into *his* service. The great assault and the temptation to apostasy has been warded off. From now on, the true sovereignty enters irresistibly on its triumphal progress. Satan, who must leave the field beaten, cannot change things any more. Jesus will drive out demons, conquer evil, and seal in his own death the defeat of Satan. Everywhere that we—united with Jesus—put our confidence only and radically in God, the same thing takes place: the might of Satan is broken and the true kingship asserted.

The Beginning of the Ministry (4:12–17)

Verses 13–16 are more or less independent and must be detached from verse 12. In verse 12 one has the impression that Jesus starts out from the Jordan region where the Baptist was staying to make for Galilee in the north. But verses 13–16 give the impression that he starts out from his home in Nazareth to settle down in Capernaum. The first statement is due to the corresponding sentence in Mark

(1 : 14), the second corresponds to the geographical picture which St. Matthew has before his mind.

¹²Hearing then that John had been handed over he retired to Galilee. ¹³And leaving Nazareth, he went and dwelt in Capernaum by the sea in the region of Zebulun and Naphtali.

The destiny of John the Baptist is accomplished. He is arrested and put in prison. The events which led up to his arrest will only be described later (14 : 3–12). In Matthew, this seems to have been actually the signal for Jesus to begin his activity. It also shows the seam which both divides and holds them together : first the Baptist does his work of " preparing the way of the Lord " (3 : 3), then Jesus starts his work. But something more than the succession in time is meant to be noticed. The Baptist is forerunner, not just in time sequence, but also in his prophetic destiny. St. Matthew uses the phrase " handed over." The same words are used later to say of Jesus that he will be handed over to the high priests and to death (20 : 18f.; 26 : 2). It is a fixed formula by which the innocence of the prisoner is indicated, and also the fact that his arrest corresponds to the will of God (who " gives him up "). The destiny of the prophets will also be accomplished in Jesus. John is his forerunner in death as well as preaching.

Jesus goes away " to Galilee," apparently to escape the same fate; but above all, because first and foremost this is to be the place fixed by God for his work. Galilee, and Nazareth in particular, had already been explained in the prelude (2 : 22f.) by means of the scriptures. Matthew names Capernaum as Jesus' domicile. By this he expresses again something more than an historical detail. For this town lies within the original tribal boundaries of Zebulun and Naphtali, which are mentioned in the quotation which follows (see Josh. 19 : 10–16, 32–39). But Capernaum also appears in Matthew as the type of the city favored by grace. In it the light dawns; beyond all others it was granted the sight of miracles. And still it was not converted. Therefore, judgment had to be pronounced on it: " And you, Capernaum, have you not been exalted to heaven? You will be cast down even to Hades. For if in Sodom had been performed the miracles that have been wrought in you, it would have been standing to this day. Therefore, I tell you : on the day of judgment it will be more bearable for Sodom than for you " (11 : 23f.). His first home town, Nazareth, pronounced judgment upon itself, because it refused to believe its native son, and so he worked no miracles there (13 : 54–58). His second home town, Capernaum, is threatened with judgment by Jesus, because it saw the signs he gave but was not converted.

[13]*This was to fulfill the prophecy which was uttered by the prophet Isaiah:* [14]*" Land of Zebulun and land of Naphtali, the way by the sea, beyond the Jordan, Galilee of the heathen—* [16]*the people that sat in darkness saw a great light, and on those who sat in the land and the shadows of death, a light has dawned."*

Once more it is the word of a prophet which the evangelist sees being fulfilled. Once when the northern kingdom, of which Galilee formed a part, was conquered by the Assyrians (722 B.C.), God brought shame upon the land of Zebulun and Naphtali. But he will make it honorable once more, when the salvation of God commences (Is. 8 : 23). Actually, the words which follow about light in darkness are to be referred in Isaiah to the whole people, not only to those who dwell in Galilee. St. Matthew understands them in the sense that it is precisely here, in the places actually named by the prophet, that the light has dawned. He chooses only a few key words from the whole text (Is. 8 : 23) which hold good for the cities where Jesus worked: " Land of Zebulun and land of Naphtali, the way by the sea " (or: the district towards the sea). The evangelist is undoubtedly not thinking of the Mediterranean, like Isaiah, but of the Sea of Galilee, called the Lake of Genesareth or also the Lake of Tiberias, on whose west bank lay Capernaum. The land " beyond the Jordan " is the land east of Jordan (Perea); in a broader sense, the region of the Ten Cities (the Decapolis) which lay to the north of this, and which bounded the Lake of Genesareth to the east—a district where Jesus often stayed (see 8 : 18.28). Most important of all, however, is " Galilee of the heathen "! This gives the character of the whole country which has been described by a series of key words: it was a loosely connected territory of mixed population, inhabited by many heathens and more or less isolated with regard to Judea, even in religious customs and doctrinal traditions. And then here, too, the " heathens " are mentioned. The representatives of the eastern world had already come to pay homage (2 : 1–12), now the theme is echoed once more.

A great light appears in the darkness. His own people do not know the way and sit in the dark. What is this light that now shines out? The coming of Jesus in general, or his doctrine, or his miracles? All these at once! Jesus is the light (Jn. 8 : 12), he brings the light, he teaches all truth, and opens the eyes of the blind. Above all, his word testifies to the light.

[17]From then on, Jesus began to preach and to say: " Repent! For the kingdom of heaven is at hand!"

Everything in the life of the Lord has its preordained time and a place fixed for it by God. The new place is Capernaum, of which the prophet spoke in his oracle; the time is the period after the dispute between himself and Satan in the desert. The first thing is the preaching, the proclamation, the word. Jesus comes as the very word of the Father; the word is the first gift he bestows. In fact, as when speaking of the Baptist, the evangelist uses the challenging word " to proclaim " to describe this " preaching." It implies a summons, the call of a herald, and a message which stirs and awakens the heart, not merely a new doctrine. It implies a message from God, which must be irrevocably delivered and at a certain hour. All this is implied here in the word " to preach." The message must be heard, not as one listens to an instruction, not even as one listens to the revelation of a truth, but as though the whole man felt himself summoned and stirred in all the movements and powers of his heart, in full readiness to let his life be created anew.

The content of the herald's cry is: " Repent! For the kingdom of heaven is at hand." We have seen that the Baptist had already used the same words. But that was only an anticipation (of the evangelist), the objective summary and interpretation of his preaching and work. The Christian was thereby informed that John already belonged to the time in which the kingship of God is announced and realized.

But now the real thing comes, the authoritative, so to speak, and efficacious proclamation itself. The former is like the shadow, the latter like the thing itself. In John's call, the emphasis was on the " Repent!" as befitted his role of precursor and preacher of judgment. The emphasis is now on the second member: " The kingship of God is at hand." This is above all a joyful word, a word of immense delight: God's unfailing will to save, all that the people of Israel longed for, all that the world hoped for: these things are now nigh at hand.

The phrase " is at hand " says two things. One is the coming of the kingship. It is not predicted in general for some time in the future, it is announced at the present moment. It comes and it cannot be stopped. But it is not said that the kingship of God is *now there*. It does not yet intervene to the full extent of its power and majesty.

Rather, the second thing is also true which is asserted in the phrase " it is at hand." It stands as it were at the door, under the walls of the city of man, on the edge of history. Its nearness is at once menacing and stimulating, but it is still only nearness. It will not do violence to men and nations; it will not force them. God is coming—but not without being expected by men and willingly accepted. To the word from on high corresponds the answer from below. That is why the call to penance, repent, precedes the call to salvation. It seems that only when this is done will the kingship be entirely there. God acts first and intervenes beforehand, but man must act and follow after. There is no coming of God without transformation of life, no kingship of God without the dethronement of man.

The First Disciples (4:18–22)

[18]*As he was walking by the Sea of Galilee, he saw two brothers. Simon, who is called Peter, and Andrew, his brother, casting a net in the lake, for they were fishermen.* [19]*And he said to them: " Come, follow me, and I will make you fishers of men." And they left their nets at once and followed him.*

The first deed recounted about Jesus' ministry is not a great miracle, not an impressive demonstration of power, but some-

thing quite ordinary. Note that St. Matthew speaks of fishermen as though they were already well-known people. Simon is
said to have the surname " Peter," Rock, which is at the same
time his official title. The author adds that Andrew is his brother.
In the various lists which give the names of the apostles, these
two are always at the beginning, Peter always first. This recalls
Simon's distinction of being the first called—which already points
to the leading place which he will later take. There is no greeting,
conversation, or " get-together," but only a summons. The point
of the order is added at once: " I will make you fishers of men."
What means they are to use, and what the object of their quest
is, is left an open question. For a long time, these men will have
no idea of what is intended. Full understanding will only come
after the resurrection of Jesus, when they are sent out into the
world to teach all nations (28 : 16–20). Now there is only a sort of
headline; but here we see that there will be two distinctive marks:
" follow me," which means unconditional attachment to Jesus;
and " fishers of men," which indicates their duty towards the
world.

The two of them follow the call immediately, dropping their
work, abandoning their livelihood, breaking the ties to wives and
families, house and homeland. Much later, years maybe, Peter
will ask about reward: " Look, we have given up everything to
follow you " (19 : 27). Jesus made renunciation of possessions and
detachment from goods a fundamental law for his disciples: " So
also none of you who does not renounce all that he possesses can
be a disciple of mine " (Lk. 14 : 33).

St. Matthew does not say, " they went with him," or " they
joined him " but, more significantly, " they followed him." This
says more than that they accompanied him as escorts for his
travels or as a group of helpers in his service. The relationship is

that of a body of followers: he is the one that goes ahead, they are the followers who come after; he is the leader, they are the led; he is the first, they are the walkers in his footsteps. This is how the relationship between them was established from the beginning, and this is how they exercised it ever more deeply in their lives until it became a following after in service, in humiliation, in persecution, and even in death.

21 And going on from there, he saw two other brothers, James the son of Zebedee, and his brother John, who were in a boat with their father Zebedee, putting their nets in order, and he called them. 22 Immediately they left the boat and their father, and followed him.

The same scene is repeated with another pair of brothers, " James the son of Zebedee, and his brother John." In the very same way as the first two, they leave their work, " the boat and their father," and join him. Not even the least hint is given of what the father thought at this moment, or how he explained to himself the enigmatic conduct of the passerby who called out and his two sons who responded. Everything is concentrated in the mighty, forceful call of him who, having been filled with the Holy Spirit, and tested in the desert, has now begun to deliver his great message and to act in the authority of his office.

Why, may we ask, does the gospel speak precisely of this at the beginning? What has it to do with the message about the imminence of the kingship of God which has just been proclaimed? Here it begins in what is without doubt an extremely modest way. These are very simple men, at least as regards their background and origins. They do not belong to the cultured or influential levels of society—and they are very few. But Jesus begins with them, and as it were, stakes everything on them. They are to be the foundation on which the building is to rise. What a venture! But Jesus knows that what he has proclaimed cannot come to grief. God's decision and his own mission are irrevocable. The work will succeed, the building will rise.

But is human liberty really safeguarded by such a call? Does not Jesus deprive these men of the possibility of weighing matters and thinking them over prudently, of making a free decision and of acting without being under pressure? They could have decided otherwise, they could have refused the call like the young man (19:16–22), or made cautious objections like others who were called (8:18–22). But they act instantly and resolutely. That is possible only because they have lived in a state of constant readiness for the call of God and for his sovereign will. But further: though they are the beginnings of the kingship of God, they have up to this not done penance; they have not changed their lives. And yet the two things are intimately connected. Here it is clear that a very special way is marked out for those who will later be called " apostles." For them, the beginning of a new life does not merely consist of a change of heart and action, but above all in the following of the Master. The beginning of their conversion is in their case linked with the immediate presence of Jesus and the common sharing of his life. In the course of the gospel we shall learn a lot more about how these beginnings were brought to a conclusion from unconditional readiness to the actual experience of following Christ, and how repentance and the new way of looking at things was practiced in this group. God has set the same goal before all: his kingship. But the ways of attainment are different: " And in the community God has appointed first apostles, second prophets, third teachers . . . are then all

apostles, all prophets, all teachers? (1 Cor. 12:28-29). Each one
must know and go his own way when he is called.

Working as Saviour in Galilee (4:23-25)

The evangelist adds to the call of the first disciples a general description of the activity of Jesus. The theater is "the whole of Galilee,"
and the Messiah is "proclaiming" and "healing." This passage concludes, on the one hand, the account of the beginning of the messianic
work, and on the other hand, leads up to the great doctrinal section of
the Sermon on the Mount which comprises the next three chapters.

²³*And he went about the whole of Galilee, teaching in their synagogues, proclaiming the good news of the kingship, and healing
every sickness and every infirmity among the people.*

Jesus had indeed taken up residence in Capernaum (4:13), but
he does not stay there. He travels around and wanders through
the land. The seed of the word must be scattered abroad; the
message must be carried everywhere. "Your word became a
delight to me; it became for me the joy of my heart" (Jer. 15:16).
The word must multiply and spread out over the land. There
must be no one whom it has not reached; "'Is not my word like
a fire, and like a hammer that breaks rocks in pieces?' says the
Lord" (Jer. 23:29).

The Messiah brings not only the word of salvation, he also
brings the work of salvation. Salvation and healing are closely
connected. It becomes clear that God brings about what is good,
what is healthy and whole. The very fact that both activities,
teaching and healing, are mentioned together in one sentence
makes it clear that both form part of the one charge given by

God. It is not merely human compassion or even the divine mercy towards the sick that urges Jesus to heal; it is the proclamation of the kingdom of God in action. Where God reaches, there the world becomes well and whole; where the Messiah appears, there sicknesses and " all infirmities among the people " are removed.

Two things are said about the message : Jesus " teaches " and " proclaims." He passes through the land, but not like a sectarian traveling preacher and healer. Rather, he teaches " in their synagogues "; he deliberately puts himself into the established order. The synagogue is the official seat of the local Jewish community where scripture is read out and explained and where prayer is offered. Jesus teaches in these places of reunion and prayer which were built in every village as a substitute for the temple in Jerusalem. The evangelist speaks of their synagogues and thereby shows how far the Jewish people and the Christian church were estranged later on when the gospel was written. Christians then felt themselves no longer at home in the synagogue, as they had for a long time in the primitive church at Jerusalem. Now they looked on those houses only as Jewish institutions from which Christians have been expelled. The painful division between Christian and Jew shows through in such places as this and moves us deeply also.

But what Jesus does in the synagogue is not to give the conventional and standard interpretation of scriptural texts and their application to the present day. Even in the synagogues Jesus " proclaims the kingdom of God." This is a festival, a time of joy, for God draws nigh, as the prophet perceived : " Sing for joy, O daughter of Sion, shout for joy, O Israel! Rejoice and be glad with all your heart, O daughter of Jerusalem. The Lord is King in your midst, you shall have no more sadness. On that day they will say to Jerusalem : ' Fear not, O Sion, let not your hands hang down! The Lord your God is in your midst, the hero, who gives victory. He rejoices over you in gladness, he renews you in his love, he exults on your behalf with jubilation ' " (Zeph. 3:14–17). When we hear or read the gospel, this joy should touch and move us.

²⁴And his fame went abroad through all Syria, and people brought to him all who were sick from various diseases and tormented by pain, the possessed and the epileptics and the paralyzed, and he healed them.

The news of the miracle worker and his teaching spread everywhere, " into all Syria," as the evangelist says. Syria is the broader northern extension of Palestine. It is his activity as healer that attracts people; so they bring to him the sick and suffering. The sicknesses are first mentioned in general, and then some are added which were thought to be very grave, and according to the minds of the ancient world, only curable with great difficulty; these were possession by the devil, " lunacy," lameness. This is a brief anticipatory summary of what the evangelist is going to present later in fuller healing narratives. An impressive picture of the might of the wonder worker and his power over all suffering is put before our eyes. It is as though a magnet were drawing to itself all tribulation and sickness, everything harmful and painful, the scourges of tormented mankind. And it is at the same time the picture of a mighty hope awakening in the hearts of men.

²⁵And great crowds followed him from Galilee and the Decapolis and Jerusalem and Judea and from beyond the Jordan.

The picture of Jesus' activity includes a third element: great crowds followed him. Not only the disciples whom he himself had gathered, but many others joined him on his travels: serious searchers after the truth, sensation seekers with nothing else to do, men and women, educated people and simple souls, the well and the ill. They hover around him like a swarm of bees, attentive to every word and gesture, trying to miss nothing, and yet impelled inwardly by a great expectation for which the word would be the "kingdom of God."

It is a company drawn from all Palestine, of which St. Matthew names the various districts: Galilee in the north, the almost totally heathen district of "the Ten Towns" (Decapolis) to the northeast of the Jordan, then Jerusalem and Judea in the south, and finally the region lying to the southeast of the Jordan (" beyond the Jordan "). This is Greater Palestine (only Samaria is not mentioned) insofar as it was still inhabited by Jews to any extent, even though they often formed a small minority among heathens. It is the same region of which the twelve tribes of Israel took possession under Joshua's leadership when they came in from Egypt and the desert. Politically, it was united only for one period in its long history: under David and Solomon. But from the religious point of view, it is the land of the patriarchs, of the promise, and remained the holy "Land of Israel" which had been allotted to the people by God. It is of this land that the Messiah now takes possession, and it of him. The way of God leads surely to its goal. From the land and people of the twelve tribes the people of God will arise anew.

The Doctrine of the True Justice (5:1—7:29)

Great " discourses " give a characteristic stamp to the gospel of St. Matthew in a very special way. Some theme from the preaching of

Jesus takes the central place in each of them. The first and most important of these discourses is the " Sermon on the Mount." In it the foundations of the messianic " kingdom " are laid. From the earliest days of Christianity down to our own times these three chapters have been like a blazing hearth from which the fire of the gospel has been enkindled in numberless hearts. We come to it as though we were entering a cathedral built of mighty stones. It is " the gospel of the gospel."

The Introduction (5:1–2)

¹*But when he saw the crowds he went up on the mountain, and when he had seated himself his disciples gathered round him. ²And he opened his mouth and taught them, saying:*

The discourse to follow is meant for the whole land of Israel : it is directed to representatives in the crowd of every tribe and region. This in itself underlines the importance of the sermon. Its importance is heightened by the fact that Jesus " goes up on the mountain " and seats himself there. A mountain is traditionally the place of divine instruction. Thus Esdras, when he read out the Book of the Law before the people, stood " higher than all the people " (Neh. 8:5). To be seated is the posture of the teacher. Thus the rabbis sat on the chair of Moses in the synagogues (23: 2), and in St. Peter's in Rome one can see St. Peter sitting and teaching *ex cathedra*, with his right hand raised to teach. In ancient Christian art Christ is often represented in the same way. What we are going to hear is not so much " preaching " as doctrine, doctrine put forward with authority and by virtue of God's mandate.

The discourse is directed to all Israel—but also to " his disciples." They are given particular mention; they draw nigh to him. This is the beginning of the Israel which is newly awakened and called together out of the twelve tribes. The collocation of "the people" and "the disciples" is not to be understood as though certain portions of the discourse were for the general public while other parts were reserved for the disciples. Nor does it mean that the words were addressed only to the disciples with the masses acting only as spectators. Rather, Jesus speaks to the disciples as to the true Israel which is already present and to the whole gathering as to the Israel of the future, the Israel which is hoped for. Or we might put it the other way round: Jesus speaks to all his hearers of the true will of God, which they must all perform, but which the disciples have already begun to perform. It is not a sermon for the pious and generous, but for all who are called to discipleship, for the "Israel" which God really wills to have, to which all should belong, even ourselves. So every word is directed to us, and there is no possibility of avoiding the great challenge.

The Call to Discipleship (5:3-16)

THE BEATITUDES (5:3-12)

The sermon begins with a "blessed" repeated eight times. This is an exclamation, a pledge, a heartfelt greeting with the sense of "well for you." It is used in the Old Testament to wish and call down upon others blessing, peace, and happiness. The opposite would be to call down a curse with the cry, "woe to you!" The cry promises welfare or catastrophe, good or evil, happiness or misery to somebody. St. Matthew opens the discourse with a long series of such blessings, while a still longer row of "woes" against the "scribes and Pharisees" is found in chapter 23. Here the beatitudes give a picture of the true people of God, and so of each individual who has been chosen by God. There the woes pass judgment on the apostate Israel, and on each individual who refuses to recognize and do the will of God.

The eight beatitudes taken together give the picture of the perfect disciple of Jesus. It will be painted in more detail in the rest of the Sermon on the Mount. We could already use as a heading here what we shall read later at an important point in the sermon: " Be you therefore perfect, as your heavenly Father is perfect " (5:48).

[3]" *Blessed are the poor in spirit, for theirs is the kingdom of heaven.*"

Jesus was sent " to bring good tidings to the poor " (Is. 61:1). At first the poor were not at all highly esteemed in the Old Testament. Property and riches were considered much more the sign of God's blessing. In later times, however, it was recognized ever more clearly that the destitute and the deprived could be especially close to God. The experience of such men may have confirmed this. Thus we find, especially in the psalms, a picture of the poor man, who is God's favorite and particularly close to his grace. This " poor man " is one who has learned to see his destiny in a new light. He does not feel himself neglected or in misery. His want of earthly goods becomes for him riches in spiritual benefits, freedom before God, humility, expectation.

These are the poor of whom Jesus speaks. They do not quarrel with their lot or think of violent upheavals. They are not in any way simple, limited, or inadequate to life, but poor " in spirit ": their poverty has a " spiritual " side. They use their lowly place in human society to interpret their relationship to God; they look to him for all things. They do not build on their own possessions in the line of righteousness and piety. Thereby their whole life has become poor—their natural and their spiritual life.

It is to these spiritually poor that the kingdom of God is promised. Indeed, they are the only ones, properly speaking, who can
ever receive it because they contribute nothing themselves but
hope for everything from on high. They are free from the weight
of earthly possessions and the weight of their own pretensions,
and thereby free for God. Everyone who wishes to enter the kingdom of God must be poor; it can only be an entirely free gift for
such as these.

⁴" *Blessed are they that mourn, for they shall be comforted.*"

Just as the Messiah is to bring good tidings to the poor, he is also
to " bind up the brokenhearted " and to proclaim the hour
" when all the mourners shall be comforted " (Is. 61 : 1f.). These
mourners are more or less the same as the " poor in spirit ": all
those who lay before God the silent anxieties of their heart and
the cry of their piercing pain. There is weeping for the loss of a
dear one, for loss of possessions or even of status, for disappointments and " outrageous fortune "; but behind it all there is a
great tribulation. It is for a world lost and ruined that they weep,
for the fact that God and his law do not prevail—a grief that
holds within it every individual sadness. This is the grief that
every man feels who is awake and his eyes open. He does not see
only his own personal destiny with all its hardships, but a universal sadness, a whole world suffering and bewildered.

But the disciples should not be men who bring troubled eyes
and gloomy faces and hanging heads to view the world. They
accept the fact of suffering. They neither pine away under it
nor toss it off with a flippant jest. They open their heavy hearts
to God. And God will comfort them, even now, since it is the
long-awaited " consolation of Israel " (Lk. 2 : 25) who utters the

liberating promise; and they will be consoled above all when God himself "wipes away all tears from their eyes, and death will be no more, nor grief nor mourning nor tribulation" (Rev. 21 : 4).

⁵" Blessed are the meek, for they shall possess the land."

We read almost the same words in Psalm 36:11 : "The meek shall possess the land." The " poor " and the " meek " are closely connected in the Old Testament. Both are frugal and poor, but resigned to God's will and full of expectation of his mercy. They oppress and exploit nobody, nor do they aim at savage vengeance or gaining their ends by violence. They know that God hates social injustice and condemns the proud oppressor : " Because they sell the innocent for silver and the poor for a pair of shoes. They tread into the dust the head of the lowly and push the miserable aside. They lie down at each altar upon garments taken as pledges, and drink the wine of the penalized in the house of their God " (Amos 2:6–8). The meek also know that God "will judge the poor with justice, and pronounce judgment for the needy in the land with equity" (Is. 11:4). These are the modest, the yielding, but still wholly open for God.

These will " possess the land." What land is meant? Primarily, the land of promise, Canaan, which the Israelites kept longingly before their eyes in the desert, and which they then received from God as his gracious gift. The land was profaned by idolatry and apostasy; it was lost to the empire of Babylon, it was granted to them once more after the captivity. But in the whole history of the people its possession never really seemed assured. In the catastrophe of A.D. 70, it was conquered and

dominated once more by the Romans. With this the unity
between God, people, and land was finally broken. Long before
that, the hope had been spiritualized. The land had become an
image for the imperishable heritage of heaven. So the yearning lives on, even beyond the New Testament, even into the
future of the kingdom of God. The land, meaning room to
live, also belongs to every man and to every nation. " He who
can call no piece of land his own is not a man," said the scribes.
The unity between God, people, and land will come, but in a
new and quite different form. It will not be conquerors and
despots who possess the land, but the lowly, the meek, and the
" silent in the land."

[6]" *Blessed are they that hunger and thirst after justice, for they
shall be filled.*"

Hunger in the world! Surely no age has ever recognized it so
keenly or suffered from it so direly as our own. Hunger is like a
cry that goes up from humanity, a human need which haunts us
in a thousand grievous images and figures. Their fill is promised
to the hungry but a complete satisfaction which will last and no
more give way to any want. This, too, is not for now but only at
the coming of the kingdom of God. Later, Jesus will underline
this word even more clearly by his action in the miraculous dis-
tribution of bread (14:13–21; 15:32–39). The important thing,
however, is that the hungry, like the " poor " and the " meek,"
are people who put their lives confidently into the hands of God
and hope for his help in time of need.

But bodily hunger is only one aspect of human hunger. The
cry for bread is a cry of the whole man. Even when the body has
been satisfied, there still remains another hunger and thirst which

is just as tormenting; indeed, it can be still more racking. It is the heart's hunger to be such as God created us and wants us to be. This is the hunger of which the beatitude speaks. Satisfaction is promised to those who "hunger and thirst after justice." It is not the legal justice of the courts, nor the practice of justice in our daily social life which we often miss so bitterly. Justice is rather to be understood in the sense in which Joseph was called just. It is what makes a man perfect before God, it is this perfection itself. Whoever wishes to be just has a passionate desire to fulfill God's will entirely and undividedly.

No indication is given as to whether this justice can also be attained by human works, or can only be the free gracious gift of God. Later texts throw more light on this question. The main thing is that such a yearning does indeed exist in man; he directs his life towards God and sees his life's highest good in the justice that makes him worthy of God. One thing is certainly affirmed: that final appeasement of his hunger, the deepest contentment of human nature, does not take place here, but in the future. This is not an escape from reality or a paralysis of human activity, but the sober acknowledgement of the truth that man does not live by bread alone (see 4:4).

[7]*" Blessed are the merciful, for they shall obtain mercy."*

Jesus assigns the kingdom of God to the poor in spirit, the mourners, the meek, and those who hunger after justice. Common to all is that their life is not closed in on itself, but that by reason of their distress it looks outward. All of them feel their inadequacy, their dependence, their weakness, the incompleteness of their lives. So, too, with the merciful. They are called blessed because they do good, place mercy above their rights, take no hostile stand against their fellow men, but try to soothe pain and heal wounds. And this is not because they are mild and kindly by disposition, but because they know that they themselves must rely on the mercy of God and live in constant dependence on him. They do not judge, so that they be not judged themselves (7 : 1); they do not requite evil with evil because they themselves have been requited only with good; they do not condemn their brother because they themselves are not condemned; they forgive those who do them wrong because they themselves are constantly experiencing God's forgiveness (see 6 : 14f.; 18 : 35). But above all : the day of judgment will come, when they, without this mercy, will not be able to stand. Just as for the stilling of hunger and the possession of the " land," their yearning, too, is for the great mercy of the day of judgment.

[8]*" Blessed are the pure of heart, for they shall see God."*

We not only hunger and thirst after justice, but also, and much more deeply, we long to see God. The whole world and its majesty is indeed only a mirror of the beauty of God. The traces of God are engraved everywhere : in the shining brilliance of the sun, the simply brightness of the flowers, the face of a child. But we do not see God himself. As the Israelite went up to the temple on Mount Sion, he had a longing to see God : " My soul thirsts for God, for the living God. When shall I come and see the face of God?" (Ps. 42 [41] : 3). " Moses said to the Lord : ' Let me see your glory, I pray you!' And he said : ' I will let all my majesty pass before your sight, and I will call out the name of the Lord before you. And I will be gracious to whom I will, and I will show mercy to whom I will.' And he also said : ' You cannot see my face, for no man shall see me and live.' And the Lord said: ' See, there is a place beside me for you to stand upon the rock. And when my glory goes by, I will place you in a cleft of the rock, and I will cover you with my hand till I am gone by. Then I will take away my hand, so that you can see me from behind: but my face you shall not see ' " (Ex. 33:18–23). Thus the prayer of Moses is only partly heard. Here on earth, the vision of God is denied us; it is reserved for eternity. " No man has ever seen him or can see him " (1 Tim. 6:16). But one day when the miracle will take place he will be visible to our transfigured eyes.

Not all will see God, but only those who are " pure of heart." That means an inmost purity and clarity, like a perfectly clean and transparent vessel for the fullness of that light. All sorts of sins render the heart impure: " What comes out of the mouth proceeds from the heart; and that is what defiles a man. For out of the heart come evil thoughts, murder, adultery, fornication, theft, perjury, and blasphemy " (15:18f.). Evil is born in the heart. The heart is thereby defiled and so the whole man (see 6:22f.). Pure of heart, however, are those from whom good proceeds, thoughts of love and mercy, desire for God and his justice. Such desires will be fulfilled when God gives himself to our eyes, to overwhelm us with bliss.

⁹" *Blessed are the peacemakers, for they shall be called sons of God.*"

God is the God of peace, he thinks " thoughts of peace, not of destruction " (Jer. 29:11). He has within him the fullness of life, but no divisions or contradictions. In our world, however, and in human society there is strife and the noise of quarrel. Unity has been torn asunder, peace has been shattered. It is not a question only of a gentle disposition, tolerance, readiness to give way. Peace is a higher thing, ultimately a divine blessing, like justice and truth, a gift of salvation, which each man is to pass on. So our effort must be to strive after a peace which embraces God, where men are in harmony with one another and with God. When this is not the case, discord may go so far as to separate parents and children and spouses, " and the members of a man's own household are his enemies " (see 10 : 35ff.).

Blessed are they who bring about peace, who reconcile adversaries, who quench hatred, who unite the sundered: in normal everyday life, with a tiny gesture, a reconciling word—but from a heart that is full of God. Blessed are they who with a pure intention work so anxiously and carefully for peace among peoples. Blessed above all are they who establish peace between God and man. That is the special task of every apostolic service, which is indeed basically, as St. Paul puts it, " the service of reconciliation " and the " message of reconciliation " (2 Cor. 5 : 18–21). But this is in fact true of every Christian. Whoever radiates the peace which he himself has in God need not use many words: he will provide a way, a bridge, for many in turn to find this peace.

At the end of time, they will all be called " children of God." That means that they will be children of God. Jesus is always finding new images to describe what life will be in the fullness of the kingship: the possession of the land, stilling of hunger, vision of God, sonship of God. The Old Testament gives the name of " sons of God " to angels and heavenly beings, but seldom to men. The title was reserved for certain exalted personages, but particularly for the kings of Israel. The future Messiah is also described as Son in the prophetic expectation: " You are my Son, this day have I begotten you " (Ps. 2:7); and at the baptism, the Father acknowledges his " beloved Son " in the same words (Lk. 3:22). This sonship of the Messiah is unique and incomparable. But the other sonship shall be the blessing of the salvation conferred on all in eternity. This is the most beautiful image of our election and our call. It implies complete fellowship with God, personal love like that between father and child, familiar nearness to the Lord of all, indeed " relationship " with God the holy. Something of what is promised for the future is already realized. Not yet in the full sense, but still really and truly, we can say: " We are called, and indeed we are, children of God " (1 Jn. 3:1).

[10]" *Blessed are they that are persecuted for the sake of justice, for theirs is the kingdom of heaven.*"

There has been persecution in all ages, loosed by personal enmity, racial ill-feeling, tribal or national disputes about possessions. But can there be persecution " for the sake of justice "? It is after all that justice of God, for which we should hunger and thirst (5:6), it is dedication to God and perfect purity and order of life—in the following of Jesus. Ought not this justice attract others instead of repelling them, inspire them rather than provoke them to hatred? Jesus knows, and here testifies, that even the greatest rectitude can be an occasion for enmity. John the Baptist was arrested and went to his death for it (4:12; see 14:3-12). Jesus will experience it himself in his own destiny. So it can also be true of those who are his disciples.

But they are blessed! Their future exaltation will be in complete contrast to their present humiliation. All who have suffered the disgrace and pain of persecution for the sake of that justice will enter the kingdom of God. Though in their earthly life nothing may be seen outwardly of their glory, still, that promise stands firm and is assured by the word of the Lord. It will lighten and lift up the hearts of many who are flagging and tiring.

[11]" *Blessed are you, when men revile you and persecute you and speak all sorts of evil against you falsely for my sake.* [12]*Be glad and rejoice, for your reward is great in heaven; for so have they persecuted the prophets before you.*"

The last beatitude does not quite fit into the framework. The dispassionate third person : " Blessed are they . . ." is replaced by the more familiar address in the second person : " Blessed are you . . ." The final beatitude is also considerably more comprehensive than the foregoing. It links up with the theme of persecution in verse 10, and strengthens the " Blessed " by the added summons to " be glad and rejoice."

Persecuted for justice's sake—*persecuted for my sake*—stand one beside the other and clarify each other. For true justice is only to be attained by way of Jesus Christ and his teaching. And vice versa: anyone who suffers persecution for his sake is thereby also persecuted for justice's sake. There is no break between the Old Testament and the teaching of Jesus; a complete unity obtains. Even Pharisees or scribes could not play off the justice of the Old Testament and their own doctrine against the teaching of Jesus.

There are many forms of hostility: insults, calumny, indeed " all sorts of evil " will be heaped on them. That will all happen to them, but it will be lying inventions. When Jesus stands before the Sanhedrin, when he is reviled and jeered at even under the cross, the disciples will have this constantly before their eyes and they will be no longer surprised. All this should cause them no sadness or make them complain: there should be no resentful defiance or anger, but rather joy and jubilation. Certainly not on account of all these insults and humiliations, but because their "reward is great in heaven." Jesus gives no cheap comfort for the next world; but he tells them soberly that this reward is just not to be expected in this life. Here the disciples are as exposed as he is to the powers of evil, to lies and hostility. But what is this great "reward in heaven"? It is none other than that which has already been promised in so many different forms: God himself, his royal lordship, the vision of God, the possession of the land, sonship of God.

The disciples are to be ready for this fate, not only in view of an uncertain future which lies before them, but also in view of the past history of their forefathers. Here, too, this law has already shown itself at work: " For so have they persecuted the prophets before you." Who are these persecutors? Their own ancestors who set themselves against the word of the prophets and offered them insult. The picture of the prophet Jeremiah, steeped in, and proved faithful by, suffering, is an eloquent testimony to this. The successors of these forefathers, who put Jesus on trial and then hated his disciples as they hated him, will " fill up the measure of their fathers " (see 23:32). What is meant then is persecution inflicted by the Jews. And they were in fact the first to try to choke the budding seed of the Christian message. That was the experience of the first missionaries and especially of St. Paul. There, too, a universal law is already manifest. It has been at work at all times in one place or another, as we know today after nearly two thousand years of church history, especially after the grievous days of the Nazi era. Jesus makes the disciples look back at the history of Israel; our view embraces a still longer period. That can sober us and preserve us from optimistic dreams. But the apostles actually rejoiced when they were found worthy to endure dishonor for the name of Jesus (see Acts 5:41). Would we also be capable of that?

THE SALT OF THE EARTH AND THE LIGHT OF THE WORLD (5:13–16)

The direct address in the second person, verses 11f., is now continued. Jesus employs two images to show what his disciples are: salt (v.13) and light (vv. 14f.). The passage ends with an express application (v.16).

¹³" *You are the salt of the earth. But if the salt loses its taste, what can it be salted with? It is no longer good for anything, except to be thrown out and trodden under foot by men.*"

Men use salt to give flavor to their food. Saltless food is flat and tasteless. Salt seems to put a sort of inner strength and flavor into all the nourishment that we take. Just as food needs salt, so too the earth, that is, the whole of mankind. Men are waiting to be given force and flavor. That is the vocation of the disciples. When they do everything that has been stated above: when they are poor and merciful, meek and pure of heart, agents of peace and full of joy under persecution, then they are the strength of washed-out mankind. This pure element, which comes entirely from the kingdom of God, and lives only for it, will be their inner strength.

The saying also has a warning sound. Jesus adds immediately: " But if the salt loses its taste, what can it be salted with?" The vocation can therefore languish, the strength of this

Godward life can fail. Then not only does the life of the disciple go to pieces, but with it collapses the strength meant for others. But apart from it there is no other salt. It is the one thing on which the earth depends, something irreplaceable which must be mixed into humanity. Flavorless salt is thrown away, people walk on it and that is the end of it. In this image, there is a distant gleam of lightning from the casting out of the faithless disciple. " It is thrown out ": we are reminded of the guest without the wedding garment who is ejected by the servants (see 22 : 12), and of the useless servant who buried the money of his master and is then cast out " into the exterior darkness " (see 25 : 30). No doubt it is a high and noble calling for the disciple himself and for the men to whom he should be salt. But it is also a calling which one can be false to, which can go slack and seep away in indifference and be ruined, and then become a total loss, indeed, something that must be liable to punishment.

[14]" *You are the light of the world. A city that lies on a hill cannot be hidden.* [15]*And no one lights a lamp and puts it under a bushel, but upon a lamp stand, so that it gives light to all in the house.*"

The second image is of still wider scope : " light of the world." The sun is for us the light of the world, without which we would sit in darkness and grope about in the gloom. Without its light there would be no colors, no beauty, we could not see our way or the world of things. The world needs this external light, but still more urgently it needs the inner light, right knowledge, the truth. Jesus first spoke of the salt of the earth, now he speaks of the light of the world. The second is more comprehensive. The same thing is meant in both cases, namely, the world of men and their life, the inhabited globe of living men. But the word " *kosmos,*" world, evokes even more strongly the impression of something all-embracing and total, the whole of earthly existence. What a claim this is! In the gospel of St. John Jesus says that he is " the light of the world " (Jn. 8 : 12). Here the disciples are the light of the world. That can only mean that the disciples themselves now carry the light of truth which Jesus has brought. The disciples belong to him so closely and are so completely filled by him that they themselves become light.

When the light is really there it cannot be stopped from shining, and nothing can resist its rays. Everything is illumined by it and it shines on everything. It is just the same as with a city which lies high up on a hill and can be seen from all sides, like a castle which dominates the countryside or a high church steeple which calls attention to the town from all directions. An Israelite would have thought immediately of one city which was " built on a height " (Ps. 122 : 3): Jerusalem. The image given by the prophets is kept, but its content is new. The disciples, who hunger and thirst after true justice, who have become the light of the world, will be that city which cannot be hidden. A single geographical point will no longer be regarded as bearer of salvation for the world, but living men, who bear the light within themselves. Wherever they are to be found there is also the " city on the hill."

The saying about light receives a second explanation: the housewife does not, of course, put the light under a bushel, that is, a vessel or jar used to measure meal, but upon a lamp stand. Only a fool would light a lamp and immediately render it useless by putting an upturned jar on top of it. A lamp is there to give light or it has no meaning at all. If a housewife lights a candle, it is " to give light to all in the house." Is it not the same with the disciples? Once more we find that the little word " all " is used—deliberately. The earth—the world —all: the same concept recurs, the whole of mankind. Here, however, " all that are in the house " may mean the members of the Christian household in the church more particularly. For the light is not only the light of the missions to the heathen, it is also the light of edification and good example for one's own family.

[16]" *Let your light then so shine before men that they may see your good works and so praise your Father who is in heaven.*"

In the application of the saying, something new is added—the light is good works. The disciples are not there to offer men a new outlook on the world or a philosophy or a set of practical precepts, but to show them life in action, something to be seen and heard. Is it then " good works " in the sense of Catholic piety? Alms for the poor box, mending altar linen, or fasting? It can be all that, but it is also infinitely more. The good works are simply the light that has penetrated life and been realized there. They are truth become tangible, faith become life. They are not something apart from faith or something that goes alongside it, like a tow-path along a river; nor are they one's own merits, which is often the reproach made by Protestants. The whole of our good works are Christian life in action, active precisely in work, always discharging like an active volcano. The light of the world is envisaged here at its highest candle-power, so to speak. The only light that really shines is the one which produces such works unceasingly and testifies to its own existence through them.

Any idea of one's own merits or of seeking praise like the hyprocrites is eliminated by the concluding words. The light that sends out its rays is not to have them reflected back upon itself. We are not to give light, that men may glorify our light. We are not to do our good works to gain praise for ourselves, but simply and solely so that God may be praised. The light of the disciple must be reflected back through him to its origin, " the Father of all light " (see Jas. 1 : 17). That is the last end and the deepest reason for the call of the disciple : by his whole being, by a life illumined by love, by works springing from the truth, to make God known.

The True Justice in the Fulfillment of the Law (5:17-48)

The beatitudes have already laid down the program for the new justice. In a second large section St. Matthew pursues the theme further, beginning with the law of Moses. Christianity, especially the groups which derived from Judaism, had to face at once the question of the relationship between what Jesus had proclaimed and demanded, and the law given to the fathers. Is the picture of perfection given in the beatitudes to be realized quite independently of this law? Is it a completely new doctrine? Or is it also rooted in the native soil of the divinely directed history of Israel and the law? The great passage that follows here, 5 : 17-48, gives the answer. It still treats of the true jus-tice, the perfect life. But the theme is developed from the law and from contemporary understanding of the law.

FUNDAMENTAL PRINCIPLE (5:17-20)

[17]" Do not believe that I have come to abolish the law and the prophets; I have not come to destroy, but to fulfill."

The law was given by God as a sacred ordinance for the community life of Israel. It was also given as a signpost for the individual, to direct his ethical and religious thought and action. The demands of God's will were expressed in it; his will was behind every letter. Beside the law stood the prophets. The will of God had also been expressed in their message. The two together, the law and the prophets, had a significance beyond their own day. The law was delivered solemnly to the people by Moses, and on Mount Sinai the people pledged themselves to observe it. Each prophet in his day proclaimed the demands of God in living speech. But it did not stay at the stage of word of mouth and oral message. All these utterances, "law and prophets," were committed to writing and handed on to each succeeding generation with the same binding force. As sacred writings they became the marrow of the life of the people of the covenant, and its inward norm. Can something which was so clearly from God, and which represented the will of God for centuries, now suddenly become invalid? And is it Jesus who is to abolish it, Jesus who had professed of himself that he was prepared to " fulfill all justice " (3:15)? This is unthinkable.

Jesus speaks of his sending in a way which no prophet had ever done when he uses the words, " I am come." That means having come from another; it means being the envoy of the Father. What Jesus does, is done in the Father's name and by his command. The Father, from whom the law and the prophets proceeded in the last instance, cannot send him to abolish them. To abolish means to render null and void, just as in human law an ordinance or a law can be abrogated. Nothing completely new now starts which has no connection with the old.

" I have not come to destroy, but to fulfill." The will of God and the sacred writings in which it is contained are to be " fulfilled "! The new is not totally different; rather, it is the completion of the old. Law and prophets are indeed God's revelation, but they are not yet the definitive. His will is revealed there, but not in its purest form.

The sacred books of the Old Testament have not been reduced to a sort of shadow of the salvation to come in the New Testament. They are still valid, but in their fulfillment through Jesus. He has told us definitively how the will of God is to be truly accomplished. We can no longer go back behind this fulfillment which Jesus has brought about. If we read the Old Testament we can only do it in the light of Jesus' revelation.

[18]" *For I tell you truly, that heaven and earth will sooner pass away than that one iota or hook of the law pass away—till all things are accomplished.*"

Here is a momentous comparison. The whole world will disappear before even the least part, even as little as the tiniest letter, of the law becomes invalid. The iota is the smallest letter in the Hebrew alphabet; the hooks are the marks which were put in to aid readers in copies of the sacred text. Every part of it and every letter are the sacred word of God and inviolable. They can never be set aside because it is God who has spoken in them. The words of men may be fleeting and perishable, the word of God abides forever.

But in fact, God has spoken not only in the law and through the prophets, he has also spoken " finally through his Son " (Heb. 1 : 1f.). This is his " last word," after which he utters no more with the same authority. This last word completes what went before and puts it in its true light. For although the law does indeed continue to exist, it does need to be completed. This is expressed in the following phrase: " till all things are accomplished." This means that the whole law must be brought to perfection and the process is already begun through the teaching of

Jesus. But it also means that everything there which pointed to the future, everything that was predicted, must be accomplished. Jesus not only teaches the fulfillment of the law, he also brings it in his person, his life, and his death. When all this has been realized—the perfect doctrine and the perfect fulfillment through Jesus—then everything will have been accomplished, all is truly completed.

As we read on, we must always see Jesus in this great context. He is no founder of a sect and no " religious genius," as one often hears. He is rather the last prophet, the final word of God, the definitive revealer of God's will—and so our way and our truth.

[19]" *Whoever therefore sets aside one of these commandments, even the least, and teaches men so, he shall be called the least in the kingdom of heaven; but whoever keeps them and teaches so, shall be called great in the kingdom of heaven."*

No one may dare to try to set aside as much as one single commandment of God, even though it were only a very minor one. It is simple to push aside the ancient and attribute to oneself new ideas. It is much more difficult to conform to traditional demands in such a way as to place them in a new light. We must keep even the least commandments with the same force of dedication and love! This will preserve us from the fallacy of thinking that the little things of everyday life are unimportant.

As one lives and teaches here, so shall he also be in the kingdom of God. There, too, there are great and small. Carefulness even in little things determines to some extent one's " rank " in the kingdom of heaven. As one has lived and taught, so shall one be. That holds good above all for those who have a teaching office in the church: catechists and pastors, priests and laymen.

They must not indulge in their own pet fancies and fix on an arbitrary choice among the objects of belief; they have been entrusted with the whole in which each portion, even " the least," has its importance.

[20]" *For I say to you: unless your justice far surpasses that of the scribes and Pharisees, you shall not enter into the kingdom of heaven.*"

Here we have the kernel, the main statement of the whole passage. It is a matter of justice. The scribes also seek it, above all in their studies and their teaching. Their task is to search the scriptures and inquire after the will of God. They give instruction to the people, teach the children, and so apply constantly to their present day what they have found in the books. Scribes, also called rabbis, are the official teachers in the country and in the metropolis of Jerusalem. They are also judges in minor lawsuits in the peasant communities. They " sit on the chair of Moses " (23:2) and have the " key of knowledge " (Lk. 11:52) in their hand. They seek true justice.

So too the Pharisees. They have no official function among the people but enjoy great personal influence. They are a religious group, a party which tries to follow the law with particular zeal —unyielding in religious matters, sworn enemies of the heathen occupying power. They are less interested in doctrine than in deeds, in the practical application of justice. Both groups have much at stake. We must not think lightly of what their position cost them.

Jesus seems to have something in common with both. Is he not a rabbi, a traveling teacher, who instructs his disciples in the true way? Like the Pharisees, is he not also first and foremost concerned with actions? Nonetheless, the difference from both of them is great. The whole gospel shows that clearly. Here we see him making fundamental demands on his disciples. They, too, have both groups before their eyes every day; they themselves have been instructed as children by the rabbis; and they experience in the streets and market-places the zealous religious conduct of the Pharisees. Both groups are concerned with justice. But that of his disciples must be divided from theirs as widely as heaven from earth.

In spite of their gigantic efforts, what they teach and do does not suffice. God demands more. The disciples are to " surpass them by far." It seems as though something absolutely new is meant by this justice. It is not a question of a difference of degree but of kind.

On Anger and Reconciliation (5:21-26)

[21]" *You have heard that it was said to the men of old: ' You shall not kill! And whoever kills shall be condemned in judgment '*."

Jesus starts from the instruction given by the doctors of the law. The word of God and its interpretation comes through their teaching. It is from them that his hearers have heard everything that God commanded; after all, only very few could read. They have accepted in the spirit of faith what God had once said to their forefathers. These ancestors, the generation which had made the exodus from Egypt and wandered in the desert, are the men of old to whom God had revealed himself. At the foot of Mount Sinai, having waited perseveringly in holy fear, they received God's commandment through the mouth of Moses. This word remains living throughout history, handed down from generation to generation until the days of Jesus. He himself also heard it and learned it in the synagogue.

One of the lapidary phrases of the ten commandments was: " You shall not kill." All life comes from God and is sacred. God expressly permitted men to kill only animals, thus allowing the use of flesh as food (Gen. 9:2f.). Human life remained the inviolable possession of the Godhead. " He who sheds human blood, his blood shall also be shed by men; for God has made man according to his image " (Gen. 9:6).

He who kills is to be " condemned in judgment ": he is to be judged according to the principle laid down in the covenant with Noah (Gen. 9:6). This principle was applied in a still more juridical form from the time of Moses: " If anyone kills a man, he shall be put to death; but whoever kills one of his neighbor's cattle, shall replace it—a living thing for a living thing. And whoever does an injury to his neighbor's person, shall be made to suffer the same damage that he has done—a fracture for a fracture, an eye for an eye, a tooth for a tooth. The same damage that he has done to another shall be inflicted on him " (Lev. 24:17–20). This law is meant to restrict retribution for injury to within the bounds laid down by the commandment of God, and prevent outbursts of wild vindictiveness. This principle—a life for a life, an eye for an eye—went very deep not only among the Israelites, but all over the East. The first necessarily implied the second. The judgment of God is given in human judgment.

[22a]" *But I say to you: whoever is angry with his brother shall be condemned in judgment.*"

Jesus opposes something new to the old way of thinking. It is solemnly proclaimed in a formula which sounds as though it were uttered by a lawgiver: " But I say to you." Something was said by God to the forefathers in ancient times. Now Jesus says what God wills in a new way. The indissoluble unity, the perpetually even balance of expiation corresponding to deed, of death penalty for death, is no longer upheld. The new law is: the very thought within the heart already renders a man liable to judgment—the human judgment in which God's judgment is expressed.

He who bears anger in his heart wishes all sort of evil on the other, indeed, he wishes that he had nothing to do with him, that the other did not exist for him. Is that not a sort of spiritual killing, a mentality which abhors, devalues, and rejects the other? " Everyone who hates his brother is a murderer " (1 Jn. 3:15). We see in this example how the " overflowing justice " (5:20) is to be constituted. The disciple of Jesus is to have as much fear of the anger which germinates in his heart as of killing a man. The standard of measurement has been changed; something more inward is demanded.

22b " *But whoever says to his brother ' Raka ' (' you dolt ') shall be condemned before the high court; and whoever says to his brother ' you fool ' shall be condemned to the hell of fire.*

These two examples take the basic principle further without changing it essentially or forcing us to take the whole as a three-fold progression to a climax. It is always the same thing, only applied to two different instances of anger. " Whoever says to his brother ' you dolt ' . . ." —is someone who not only nurses anger secretly in his heart, but gives vent to it in a scornful word. The word " raka " is a contemptuous insult, a jeering epithet. The disciple is to be on his guard also against using such language. It is mortally dangerous. It is not meant, and indeed it never happened, that such a man was haled before the Sanhedrin, the high court, to be condemned. What is meant is the very same as in the first example—anger renders one liable to judgment.

So too the third example, which gives another insulting word, " you fool ", you idiot. The first scornful epithet hardly differs at all from the second, at least not enough to justify so great a difference in the punishment. Rather, the latter two examples complement one another penalty-wise—the high court and the hell of fire. Whoever denounces his brother in anger and be littles his honor is juridically the same as a murderer before the court of law; but on account of his guilt in the eyes of God, on account of the sin, is like one who is ripe for hell.

The word " brother " occurs regularly. Who is this brother? The Israelites gave each other this honorable title. It was a title due to each member of the people of the covenant. A brother is a man of the same family, the same blood, the same faith. Jesus used the word mainly in this sense too. Later, when the church applied these words of Jesus to itself, it had to understand by brother the fellow believers. To be heathen or Jew, free man or slave, meant nothing any longer; all were brothers in Christ. This law is valid for the community of believers, the co-heirs of Jesus Christ. In the brotherhood of the Christian community this law must live. Here all aversions, hatred and anger must be feared and condemned. How carefully and delicately must consciences have been formed; how awful must the transgression of Jesus' command have been felt in the early church! And how powerful should be the urge in us, to strangle at the very first stage all evil against a brother!

²³" When therefore you bring your gift in sacrifice to the altar and remember that your brother has anything against you, ²⁴leave your offering there before the altar, and go first and be reconciled with your brother. And then come and offer your gift in sacrifice."

There should be nothing to divide the brothers—no aversion or quarrels. Otherwise they are not capable of worshipping God worthily. The example of the sacrifices offered in the temple clarifies the commandment of Jesus. If there is discord between the brothers, then the bond between them and God is also broken. Jesus says nothing against the offering of sacrifice which was prescribed by the ordinances of the law and was practiced as a matter of course. He is no heated adversary of formal worship and liturgical rites. In the offering of sacrifice, public for the whole people, private for the welfare of the individual, true worship of God can find expression. But there is an inexorable condition attached to it: the mind to honor God is authentic only when it arises from peace and unity with one another.

The example does not even mention a case where I have something against another—a justifiable reproach or even a grudge in the heart. But on the contrary: it is enough already to know that another has something against me. Then it is I who must take the first step towards reconciliation; I must make my way to him and restore peace. That is so urgently necessary that I must leave my offering, the well-chosen beast or the harvest fruits lying or standing before the altar. I must pay no attention to the delay in the process of the sacrifice, and pay no attention to the surprise and talk that will follow. And this I must do simply because of the sudden, terrifying consciousness that I am not at peace with a brother, and so am unworthy. Only when reconciliation has been effected am I in fit state to offer my sacrifice. Then it will be pleasing to God and will also bring about reconciliation with him. Peace with one another is the condition of peace with God.

That is really something new. The worship of God and the fact of brotherhood in daily life are closely bound up with one another. The worship offered to God is without value, if it is not sustained by brotherly love and unity. No matter how numerous and valuable are the sacrifices which one offers, they can never replace this presupposition. Jesus has here in mind the sacrificial cult of his own day. St. Mark has preserved for us an example of the practice which the doctors of the law then regarded as legitimate. There the Lord maintains the same principle: God can never find a gift pleasing which has been provided at the cost of a child's duty towards his parents (Mk. 7:9-13; Mt. 15:3-9). The danger of failing one's human and moral duties in the name of one's worship of God is always there: from the abuses which the prophets denounced to many forms of modern hypocritical piety. How gladly would we buy ourselves freedom from some difficult human relationship by the easy flight into the purely religious sphere of prayer, work or penance.

Since Jesus as high priest offered himself to God in the Holy Spirit once and for all as a well-pleasing sacrifice, this ancient sacrificial worship has been abrogated. Still, Christians also offer sacrifice, spiritual gifts, their bodies and themselves as acceptable offerings in and through the high priest Christ. With regard to these sacrifices and, above all, for their source and center, the eucharistic sacrifice in the church, the words spoken by Jesus hold good. God only accepts them when they spring from peace and charity among one another. How attentive should be our thinking in this matter! Quarrels and discord make the community unfit for the worship of God. What pains must we take, what earnestness must we summon up to effect reconciliation so that all worship of God will not become empty and meaningless!

²⁵" *Make friends with your adversary quickly, while you are still on the way with him so that your adversary may not hand you over to the judge, and the judge to the police, and you find yourself cast into prison.* ²⁶*Truly, I tell you, you will not be released from there until you have paid the last farthing.*"

Here is a second example drawn from real life. Someone owes money to a creditor and when he refuses to pay he is dragged forcibly with threats and curses before the judge. The judge upholds the creditor's claim and has the debtor led away by the servants of the court to a prison cell. He has to stay there until he has paid the money owed down to the last dime. That is what happens among men: everyone tries with the law's help to gain his rights—if necessary by applying force.

What precisely is the warning which Jesus gives? Make use of the time for reconciliation as long as you still have any prospects. While you are on the way, you are alone with your legal opponent and without witnesses. You can try anything then to come to terms with him. Perhaps you will succeed, perhaps not. But in any case you must profit by the time you have. An accord here does not seem to come under the heading of a duty of brotherliness. Isn't it a rather homely counsel of prudence?

It would be so, if the little tale did not have a serious background. Use the time before it's too late. This urgency points to another imminent event and the judge evokes another and greater judge—God in his kingship and his office of judge. We are all on the way, going to meet judgment. One can picture the consequences and almost calculate the very hour . . . And so the duty of reconciliation becomes an urgent anxiety while there is still time. Later it will be too late. Do not therefore postpone the hour, and make every possible effort to live at peace with one another.

ON ADULTERY (5:27–30)

[27]" *You have heard that it was said: you shall not commit adultery. [28]But I say to you: Everyone who gazes at a woman in order to lust after her has already committed adultery with her in his heart.*"

The sixth commandment of the decalogue is to protect marriage and render it secure. The command, " You shall not commit adultery," is of general validity and holds good for the man and the woman in the same way. But the interpretation of the law and its application by the doctors gave the husband more freedom than the wife as we shall shortly see (5:31f.). The inviolability of this union between husband and wife was assured merely by the fact that an external breach against it was forbidden, namely, consummated adultery, which represented a juridical fact disrupting the union. It is of permanent importance that marriage should be highly esteemed as a social bond, and that it be protected by the law. Peoples and states are bound to see to this themselves.

Jesus does not set aside the prohibition. But he teaches that the purity of marriage is not assured merely by this prohibition. An adulterous offence against marriage is committed as soon as lustful desire for another woman is found in the heart. The outward act is only the completion of the inward desire. Before God, what counts is the mind, the purity of thought, the unspoilt and clear will. The married man must be formed by this purity right to the roots of his thinking. If one has really done this, he will find that many social rules and church laws about the inviolability of marriage are the natural consequence. God looks into the heart; he judges us by our intention. And it can also be true that outwardly blameless conduct, which never gives offence, can still be thoroughly hypocritical. Behind the gleaming facade can lie concealed a refuse heap of inner decay and disintegration. Outside and inside, living and thinking, face and heart should correspond to one another entirely. Men who live in this way can be recognized by their eyes, the cleanness of their speech, their unfeigned actions.

[29]" But if your right eye is a scandal to you, pluck it out and cast it from you. For it is better for you, that one part of your body perish, than that your whole body be cast into hell. [30]And if your right hand is a scandal to you, cut it off and cast it from you. For it is better for you, that one part of your body perish, than that your whole body go down to hell."

These are hard words. They can only be understood when one knows what a scandal is. The word (skandalon) can mean various things. One speaks of " giving scandal " when someone leads another into sin; one speaks of " taking scandal " when one is incited to sin by something outside oneself. Among the possibilities of being guilty of sin, there is one which surpasses all others: this is the " great scandal," the real temptation, total apostasy. It is spoken of several times later. It is not intended here, where what is meant is being misled to commit particular sins, sins of sexual misconduct and moral depravation, to be precise. For Matthew has clearly linked the words to the admonition on perfect purity of heart.

Temptation does not come here from other men, but from within oneself whence spring " evil thoughts . . . adultery, fornication " (see 15 : 19). But temptation makes use of the members of one's own body. The eye and the hand are mentioned in particular; they seem to be the specially favored instruments of this scandal: the eye which gazes lustfully and covetously around; the hand which stretches out for forbidden things and tries to grasp them—as the adulterer tries to hold the wife of another. The parts of the body are not evil; nor indeed is the body itself, as has often been held by those who despised the flesh. But the members can be instruments of evil.

When temptation makes its assault, the disciple must act radically and at once throw back the first attack. This decisiveness is meant by the words, " Pluck it out and cast it from you . . . cut it off and cast it from you." In the apparently minor skirmish the whole battle is at stake. If the disciple leaves the door open a crack to sin, he will be totally overwhelmed by it; his citadel will be stormed. Sexual laxity is always followed by a weakening of the whole moral fiber, of strength of character and of earnestness in religious life. Often the way of estrangement from God begins with such defects.

What threatens the disciple who does not act decisively is " Gehenna." We translate the word by " hell." This was the

name given by the Jews of Jesus' time to the place of punishment
after the last judgment. Jesus speaks of it frequently—terrifyingly
often. Only when one is aware of this possibility, of being rejected for ever and separated from God, does our striving take
on its full seriousness. This is no game; the way of discipleship is
no easy promenade. We should certainly decide differently in
many things, if we thought of this more often, not timorously,
but in manly soberness.

The language of these two sayings is harshly realistic and deliberately hyperbolical. They are to be read in the light of v. 28;
the attitude of the heart is decisive. It is not a matter of a skirmish
on the borderline of the sinful and the permissible or in a neutral
space between the lines of battle; rather, the whole battle is at
stake. We are placed before an " Either-Or." He who has once
said an honest yes to the will of God and to the gospel will find
these words not oppressive, but rather a sort of liberation. There
is after all only one way. But we are not thrown back upon our
own feeble strength; God himself through the Holy Spirit works
in us both to will and to accomplish : " Or do you not know that
your body is a temple of the Holy Spirit who dwells in you, and
whom you have received from God, and that you do not belong
to yourselves? You have been bought at a great price. Glorify
therefore God in your body " (1 Cor. 6 : 19f.).

On Divorce (5 : 31–32)

[31]" *It was also said: A man who divorces his wife must give her a
certificate of separation.* [32]*But I say to you: Whoever divorces his
wife—except in the case of fornication—makes her commit adultery; and he who marries a divorced woman commits adultery.*"

Here we have a positive law of the Old Testament called in question. Deuteronomy 24 : 1 laid it down that a husband was justified in repudiating his wife " if he found some indecency in her," but that he had to make a documentary declaration giving her a " bill of divorce," a written statement of his wife's release from the marriage bond. This is the only case we know where Jesus abrogates a formal law of the Old Testament and replaces it with a new precept. It was precisely here where the original ordinance of God had been abandoned and the rights of the woman had been so badly infringed that the true will of God had to be brought into force once more. This the Lord does by his authority as " Fulfiller " of the law. Here it means that the old and imperfect law is being replaced by the new and perfect law. But the new is in reality the old because it corresponds to the original will of God which was expressed in the book of Genesis (1 : 26f.; 2 : 23f.) dealing with the creation of the world and of man.

Jesus forbids the husband to repudiate his wife. If he does so, she would become an adulteress when she married again—for the old bond of marriage remains in force. And vice versa : if someone marries a woman who has been divorced by her husband, he commits adultery with her because her earlier marriage still remains valid. Not just the wife, but also the husband sins, if they both contract a second marriage in spite of their being bound by an earlier one. This clear ruling has been preserved for us by the first three evangelists. St. Paul too knows it as a commandment of the Lord (1 Cor. 7 : 10f.). The church has felt itself bound by this ruling from the earliest days as an inviolable law. No power in the world, not even the church and the pope, is competent to dissolve independently what God has joined together. The rigor of church law on marriage has often been misunderstood; but its inflexibility derives from this one source, the clear ruling of the Lord and the holy will of God expressed therein. However, this ruling was given for the sake of man, for the due ordering of his life and salvation. Experience confirms this in many ways. We must not just submit to this ironclad order of things as though it were an oppressive ukase, but welcome it with our whole heart because it proclaims the truth.

ON SWEARING (5:33–37)

³³"Again you have heard that it was said to the men of old: You shall not swear falsely, you shall render to the Lord your sworn vows."

For the second time Jesus uses the longer formula of introduction: " You have heard that it was said to the men of old " (see 5:21), and thereby inaugurates a second group of examples of true justice. Here two Old Testament commandments are in question. The first refers to a solemn affirmation before God which calls him to witness to an assertion. This we call swearing. The Old Testament commandment orders not to swear falsely (Lev. 19:12). If someone turns to God and calls upon him to bear witness, what he says must be absolutely true and sincere. Otherwise he commits the blasphemy of debasing God to the service of a lie, of making him who is holy and true a false witness.

The second commandment bears on the relationship of man to God under a different aspect. If someone makes a promise to another, then the honor of both demand that this promise be kept. It is also possible to make a promise to God. The obligation is then far stronger; we call it a vow. If someone has bound himself in that way before God, he has incurred the sacred obligation of fulfilling his promise. This is inculcated by the commandment: " You shall fulfill your sworn vow to the Lord." Both times it is a matter of man's duty in face of God and reverence for the holiness of God is commanded. We are also to pay attention to this, but this is not yet enough.

³⁴" *But I say to you: Do not swear at all! Not by heaven, for it is God's throne;* ³⁵*and not by the earth, for it is his footstool; nor by Jerusalem, for it is the city of the Great King.*"

Jesus does not challenge either of these two commandments, but he does take them further and make them go deeper. It is not enough to be on one's guard only against sins and negligence with regard to God, that is, merely to avoid evil. The disciple must live in a more personal proximity to God. One who takes pains to carry out these two commandments can still offend against God's holiness. The rabbis and the Pharisees did so, often splitting hairs to find reasons. The sharp " do not swear at all " is aimed primarily against this. For in Palestine the customary manner of swearing was already a breach of the reverence due to God. They proclaimed indeed the rule that the name of God could not be uttered and could not be used in an oath or affirmation. For the name of God is holy. But it could be paraphrased: by heaven, by Jerusalem—wherein God was always meant. But this really threw the door wide open to abuses and frivolity. Jesus puts his finger on this weak spot, this pettifogging manipulation of divine things.

He says: anyone who swears " by heaven " for all practical purposes still says " God." For what else is heaven but the throne of God; as we read in Isaiah: " So says the Lord: heaven is my throne and earth my footstool. What is the house that you would build for me, and what would be my dwelling place? For my hand has made all these things " (Is. 66:1f.). It is the very same thing with " by earth." " Earth " was indeed not one of the contemporary transcriptions of the name of God. But if the earth is the stool beneath God's feet, it is then his property. So too " by Jerusalem," because God had chosen this city and Mount Sion as the place of his presence. The psalms sing its praises: " Lovely and lofty, the joy of all the earth is the mountain of Sion in the depths of the north, the city of the mighty King " (Ps. 47:3). He who light-heartedly uses the name Jerusalem to swear by is thereby doing injury to the honor of God.

[36]*Nor may you swear by your head, for you cannot turn a single hair black or white.*

The last example seems to have a touch of humour. One can imagine a vivacious Latin gesticulating violently and rolling his eyes, trying to convince someone of the truth of what he's saying, perhaps only of his cheap prices. The buyer does not believe him and accuses him of shady practice. So he takes to swearing to prove what he says: " I swear to you by my head." Why all this display? asks Jesus. You offer him your head as the price of your sincerity for a trifling matter? And all the same, you cannot make a single hair of your head either black or white; that is, you cannot either fix or change your age. Like so many other sayings of Jesus this one is full of startling simplicity and hidden profundity. For behind this saying lies the great truth that God is the Lord of your life. He has counted all the hairs of your head (10:30) and has made you as you are. How can you offer something as a pledge when you have absolutely no control over it? Do we not often toss off strong expressions like, " I swear," and " I declare to God," without thinking of what we are saying? Our speech should be so straightforward and true that we have no need of such pompousness.

³⁷" *Let your speech be: Yes, yes, no, no; anything that goes beyond that is from the evil one."*

When you speak your words must really say what is in your mind. A *yes* must be really an affirmation, a *no* must be really a denial. This is true above all when you address yourself to God, but should also be true with men. For we are always the same person, and he who is frank and loyal with God will be no different with men. Jesus is not giving just a rule of ethics; nor is he just setting up a standard for correct conduct between men. That would remain within the limits of natural philosophy, of a morality which men could reach by themselves, and which has in fact been reached by noble pagans. But it is not a matter of humanist ethics here. The word of Jesus is always uttered as a message from God. He also sees the great adversary, the evil one. The thoughtless word which juggles with the honor of God is not merely a human imperfection, it is sin : " Anything that goes beyond that is from the evil one." The evil one takes his stand for preference in the broad area that lies between the clear and precise commandment and the clear and precise prohibition. He tries to pin us down to what is merely legitimate, the letter of the law. He tries to persuade us that we have plenty of elbowroom to play with what is neither expressly forbidden nor permitted. He also likes to hide himself behind interpretations of the word of God which are smooth and unobjectionable on the surface, but are inwardly hypocritical. Are we to believe one another only when we add our affidavit or its equivalent? What matters is that we should be sincere right down to the roots of our being. After that, all accessories are superfluous.

ON RETALIATION (5:38–42)

[38]" *You have heard that it was said: An eye for an eye, a tooth for a tooth.* [39a]*But I say to you: Do not resist one who is evil.*"

Man is inclined to practice retaliation for any injustice done to him. A wild revolt often overcomes him and the urge for vengeance, and he desires to pay back the other many times over for the hurt that he himself has suffered. If one man commits a crime, the whole tribe is penalized. An injury is inflicted and the victim aims at once for the offender's life. A city is bombed, and as a measure of reprisal a thousand times as many bombs are unloaded on the enemy's city.

The wild vindictiveness of man is kept in bounds wherever the amount of retaliation has been exactly fixed. This was done in the ancient law codes of oriental nations and in the legal books of the Old Testament. The amount of punishment was to correspond to the amount of the damage and should not go beyond it without restriction. Here one of the fundamental principles of justice is laid down and strictly enforced: " But if further damage ensues, then you shall give an eye for an eye, a tooth for a tooth, a hand for a hand, a foot for a foot, a burn for a burn, a wound for a wound, a stripe for a stripe " (Ex. 21 : 23–25). It does not seem as if Jesus abolished this juridical norm of the Old Testament which meant to control the whole field of civil law. On the contrary : just as in the previous cases he is concerned with the sort of thinking which was behind the whole Israelite tradition. Here it involves insisting on one's legal claims, on revenge, being bent on strict and merciless justice, the thought that is so deeply rooted in the perverted heart of man—I will pay you back in your own coin. Whoever thinks and acts in this way may be convinced that an injustice has been completely eliminated as soon as it has gained exact satisfaction. Jesus points to another way—the way of the super abundant justice.

He sets up a new way of thinking in terms of love (in opposition to the Old Testament way of thinking in terms of justice) when he lays down the principle : " Do not resist evil." Harm is not overcome when we fight it off with a like harshness, but rather when we endure it. Evil retains its strength as long as it remains in power, where the injured person retaliates with the same weapons. But it loses its strength when it is absorbed by patient love. The blow falls on empty air and the force is wasted since it meets with no resistance. In this way alone can the might of evil be broken—by letting it dash itself in pieces against oneself.

[39b]" *But if anyone strikes you on the right cheek, turn to him the other also.* [40]*And if anyone wishes to go to law with you and take your coat, give him also your cloak.* [41]*And if anyone presses you into service for a mile, go with him two.*"

What this means is shown by three examples taken from daily life. First there is somebody who has been given a slap in the face, and hence deeply wounded in his honor. He draws back his fist to return the blow—and Jesus steps in to say : Not like that—stretch out the other cheek for him to hit you, and you will find that he stops, bewildered and at a loss, and that his anger evaporates. Even if he does strike again, it is better to put up with the injustice than to commit a new injustice.

Someone else has a legal dispute to settle and hauls the other into court by the scruff of the neck, to get possession of his coat, perhaps as a pledge or as substitute for damages. Do not struggle with him, and do not claim your rights before the judge, but let him have your cloak too. You will find that you have the same experience as before. But if not, still, you have acted as son of the heavenly Father, and you have made in your turn a gift of the love which he shows you. And love is stronger than evil.

The third has pressed you to go a mile with him, perhaps to perform forced labor, demanding that you carry a load or maybe only to show the way. Do not revolt against the imposition, bear no resentment in your heart, do not cudgel your brains to see how you can get rid of him—but go at once two miles with him. Let your kindness overcome him and so break down his will to do violence.

[42]*" Give to him that asks of you, and do not turn away from him that would borrow from you."*

A summary of the foregoing comes at the end but it envisages once more two concrete cases: not to meet a request with a refusal and not to reject a plea for a loan. Does this mean that we are to forget all prudence and foresight? Is one to become the tool of others' moods and a simpleton frivolously exploited by others? It cannot mean this. The important thing in all these cases is not the explanatory instance but the truth which the example is to illustrate. And this is: not to resist evil. That can of course be done out of cowardice, innate weakness or a feeling of inferiority; it can even be done out of a pride and self-assurance which refuses to lower itself to the level of the other. Jesus means nothing of this sort; he means a new way of thinking, the attitude of love which is opposed to evil with overwhelming force and demands supreme self-control. After all, he himself answered the man who struck him with the words: " But if I have spoken rightly, why do you strike me?" (Jn. 18:23). It is not a matter of a fundamental renunciation of one's rights and of one's honor, much less of a new juridical order in public life, but of a nobler attitude, the superabundant justice. It is the same as what Paul says to the Romans: " Do not let yourselves be overcome by evil, but overcome evil by good " (Rom. 12:21).

ON LOVE OF ENEMIES (5:43-48)

[43]" *You have heard that it was said: You shall love your neighbor and hate your enemy.*"

The command of loving one's neighbor is one of the loftiest of the Old Testament. By neighbor, of course, was meant a member of the chosen people. It must be regarded as progressive that this commandment included in many regards the stranger dwelling in the land but not belonging to the same race by blood. To a great extent the same privileges and precepts held good for the settler in their midst as for the Israelites themselves. Thus even in the Old Testament the circle of " the neighbor " is rather widely drawn. A sincere love of benevolence is ordered, which goes beyond the law, to wish and do good to the other.

But one boundary was never crossed—the line drawn between Israel and the enemy. The enemy means the enemy of the country, the armed adversary of the nation. To be sure, we nowhere read in the Old Testament that the enemy as such is to be hated. In pre-Christian times this explicit form was demanded only from the members of the sect by the Dead Sea. But the attitude of legitimate hatred is taken for granted since everybody envisaged land and people as one thing with God. An attack on land and people was always an attack on God and was met with implacable harshness. This is shown in the campaigns of conquest in the book of Joshua, in the wars of the era of the kings, in the female figures of Judith and Esther, and in the embittered struggle against the heathen rulers of the times of the Seleucids described in the books of the Maccabees. Therefore one could easily complete the precept of love of neighbor with the words: " and you must hate your enemies."

[44]" *But I say to you: Love your enemies and pray for your persecutors.*"

Although he abolished the type of thinking behind the traditional practice, once more, it is not true to say that Jesus sets aside the commandment given in the Old Testament. In private retribution the juridical way of thinking, " What you do to me, I do to you," is to be broken down. Now the division between friend and foe in public and national life is simply to be set aside as well. In the minds of the disciples the idea of " enemy " must be no more.

The love of the disciple is to reach out to all men; every individual can be his neighbor: " Love [also] your enemies and pray for your persecutors." Here we are probably not meant to think of personal enemies to any great extent, for example those who envy or slander us, the ill-intentioned neighbor or business competitor. Rather, it reminds us that even in the lifetime of Jesus his disciples suffered the hostility and the slander which Jesus was met with. How much truer it was when the mission was fully launched, and the missionaries and the Christian communities were heavily oppressed! How timely must they have felt Jesus' command: pray for your persecutors and love your enemies! They are not to respond by hatred and aversion, and thus strengthen the walls of enmity. Their task is always the same—to conquer hatred by love.

Prayer in particular is not to be offered only on behalf of those who share the one outlook. It must be comprehensive, magnanimous, and include all opponents of Christ. This way did indeed lead to a victory which was won without violence, in humility and love. It is still today the royal command of discipleship, the ripest fruit of a truly Christian disposition. How great the gain, were we to act with tranquil confidence in the fruit of such love!

⁴⁵*". . . that you may be sons of your heavenly Father; for he makes his sun shine on the wicked and the good, and his rain fall upon the just and the unjust."*

To become sons of the Father—that is the goal; not a humanism of this world, the quest for the finest possible manhood, the fulfillment of the personality. God is the model. His way of acting, the Lord tells us, is to be prodigal with his kindness. He makes the sun shine, he sends the rain without regard to the worthiness or gratitude of men. Just as they all have a share in his natural gifts, so they are all granted the riches of his grace. Our mind must correspond to his and our actions should flow from the same generous and optimistic love. We must imitate him so that in the end he recognizes and accepts us as his true children.

[46]" *For if you love (only) those that love you, what reward do you deserve? Do not the tax gatherers also do the same?* [47]*And if you greet only your brothers, what is extraordinary about that? Do not the heathen also do the same?"*

Love must surpass by far what the doctors of the law and the Pharisees preach and practice (5:20). It also goes far beyond all that can be observed among tax gatherers or pagans. *The tax gatherers* also love their fellows; they do not tear each other's eyes out. The tax officials were despised and relegated to the lowest level of officialdom. What they do is perfectly normal and there is no need to talk about it. To be polite and friendly to one another is something universal, even among the heathens who do not know the true God. But they do know the rules of human intercourse and considerate behavior. Not only should such friendly thoughtfulness be the rule among you, you must extend it to all others. At the same time, a greeting between Christians will always be particularly warm and heartfelt because it is a sharing and exchanging in the life of grace. Thus Paul often demands : " Greet all brothers with a holy kiss " (1 Thess. 5:26). The exchange of heartfelt love should not remain restricted to one's own circle, to the tried and trusty companions in the faith, to the parishioners of one's own church. All must have their share in it—the people of our street, our colleagues at work, and the many strangers with whom we come in contact every day. Jesus imparts himself to others in our love and its friendly greeting.

Jesus asks: " What reward do you deserve?" The word " reward " has been mentioned once already. A " rich reward in heaven " was promised for all the troubles of persecution and insult. Here too the gospel speaks without embarrassment of the reward which the disciple will expect. It is not the intrinsic motive of our action. God's conduct towards us, and ultimately God himself, is the only motive. But whoever lives in this sort of love and carries out the directions of the Lord will also receive the reward. It is the same as was offered to us in various images in the beatitudes: sonship of God (see on this 5 : 45), the whole fullness and blessedness of the kingdom of God, God himself. One need not be afraid of doing things for the sake of reward; for the deeper one lives in God, the more one acts for his sake in all things.

[48]" *Be you therefore perfect, as your heavenly Father is perfect.*"

This is a preliminary conclusion of the whole section from 5 : 17 on. The saying sums up what was stated as a program in 5 : 20 and then expounded by means of six examples. We meet here for the first time the word " perfect " apropos of human action— a word which only Matthew uses in this sense. What does " perfect " mean? It is a very pregnant word. The Old Testament, where it is often used, gives us the key to it. Perfection and justice correspond to one another. In the terminology of sacrifice the word gives a clear-cut concept of the undamaged state of the gift or beast offered in sacrifice. Among human beings, he is " perfect " who has directed his heart to God and fulfilled the law unflinchingly and in pure dedication. It was said of Noah that he " was a perfect and just man " (Gen. 6 : 9; see Ecclus. 44 : 17). It is the man who has made of his life something whole and compact, after having overcome everything half-hearted and fragmentary, uniquely directed towards God and to an undivided service in his sight. Of God himself it is never said that he is perfect.

But Jesus says so. The disciple must also be perfect in the way that God is. The disciple is therefore to imitate God, to reflect and express the conduct of God in his own efforts. This thought had had an exalted model in the Old Testament where the book of Leviticus laid down the principle: "You shall be holy, for I the Lord your God am holy" (Lev. 19:2). This precept demanded above all a cultic, sacral holiness (pureness) through which Israel was to become worthy of the worship of Yahweh. Something different is meant here. Man is to copy God's own being and nature, his way of thinking and his disposition, and above all his divine love. One may well be terrified at the thought.

Perfection can be properly understood only in the light of love, the essence of God. Otherwise it results in a virtuous ideal which may be Greek or Stoic or Buddhist or whatever you like, but is not what Jesus intends. Of course, we are still allowed to speak of "striving for perfection." That has been done in the church and in its traditions of spirituality down to the present day. It can mean something false if one conceives of perfection as the sum of all virtues. But it is very much to the point if one understands perfection as fulfillment in love. This demand goes far beyond anything that we ourselves could imagine or achieve. It must be God himself who awakens the urge in us; it is not so much a matter of our advancing as of God's leading us on.

As the law is "fulfilled" by Jesus, so it should be done by us (5:17). The present text sums up what we have read up to this point (5:17–47), indeed, all the precepts of the entire gospel. It explains their lofty demands: how could they be less, since it is a matter of divine conduct? Constant readiness for reconciliation, domination of sensual urges, utter sincerity, renunciation of all revenge, and even love of enemies: all this is of a divine nature. It is the highest end that can ever be set before us, but one which also corresponds to our inmost desire: we long for what is supreme and whole, half measures are not enough for us. It should be emphasized that this is no wishful thinking that has lost touch with reality. It can be attained in the grace of God. For the love which is spoken of here " has been poured out in us " by God " through his Holy Spirit " (Rom. 5:5). The thrust of this love is towards life. The life of the saints makes it manifest to all.

The True Justice in the Performance of Good Works (6:1-18)

What follows is still concerned with the true justice of 5:20. The preceding examples showed how the old law was to be fulfilled in the new spirit. Jesus now speaks of three highly prized practices of the religious life: almsgiving, prayer and fasting. True worship of God and true justice can find expression in them if they are done in the right spirit. But the opposite can also happen when they become purely external forms or even serve human selfishness. Jesus exposes hypocritical behavior and points out the right way unambiguously.

[1]" *See to it that you do not practice your justice before men to let yourselves be seen by them; otherwise you have no reward from your Father in heaven.*"

To begin with, Jesus disclosed the opposition between true and false practice of justice. Is it done for the sake of men or for God? Behind the good works is concealed a mentality which seeks only its own self-assertion. It seeks praise from its fellow men instead of acceptance by God. Instead of waiting for reward from him alone, it speculates on reward from men. Something that perhaps appears as a harmless vanity or a very human, but pardonable weakness, is in the end not in God's service, but men's. And so the whole thing becomes hollow and worthless. True worship of God can only be directed to God himself and the reward promised by him. Every side-glance towards the praise or blame of one's fellow men falsifies this pure devotion to God. It is not said that a " good work " should be done only for the sake of the divine reward, but the reward is bestowed of itself if this pure disposition is present.

ON ALMSGIVING (6:2-4)

[2]" *But when you give alms, do not have a trumpet blown before you as the hypocrites do in the synagogues and on the streets that they may be praised by men. Truly, I tell you: they have received their reward.* [3]*But when you give alms, then your left hand should not know what your right hand does* [4]*so that your alms-giving remains secret; and your Father, who (also) sees what is secret, will repay you.*"

By giving alms, one does not buy one's discharge from urgent social duties. One knows, rather, that one holds one's own possessions only in trust and that one has not been given full ownership of them. The poor and needy are as much part of the community as anyone else and they have the same rights as everybody. Care for the poor is the acid test of the presence of a proper social attitude in a people. The prophets were tireless in inculcating this on their fellow citizens. In the last resort, however, this care for those in need should not stem from human compassion and social responsibility alone. It must come from an attitude towards God. For he is the Father of all men. It is his will that no one should remain in need but that his cause should be mercifully taken up by his brothers—because God himself always has mercy on the whole people.

But even then, when someone gives alms for the sake of God he is not out of danger. Here precisely the danger of self-seeking lies in wait for him. Jesus has his eye on men who boast and brag of their expenditure, who proclaim out loud the amount of money or the value of the gift they have donated. They wish to bring home the prize of human praise and have the good name of benefactors. Their name is to be noised abroad from mouth to mouth : see how much good he does.

Jesus points back to the right way : what you do should remain a secret. When no one learns about it, indeed, when you do not notice it yourself or when you forget about it at once (" the left hand should not know what the right hand does "), then you have the assurance that your work was done for God. Do not worry about its being forgotten or finding no recognition. God sees also what is secret. There is no region inaccessible to him and he knows about the most intimate stirrings of your heart. He knows your mind exactly and weighs accordingly the value of your deed. He who seeks the praise of men does indeed have his reward at once, but it is a meager, earthly reward and he may expect no other. He has already " receipted the bill." But the other is really rewarded when he does good unobserved and simply for the sake of God.

On Prayer (6:5-15)

The next example is prayer. First Jesus speaks of prayer in the same way as alms: hypocritical prayer practiced in the sight of men and prayer offered in the spirit of true justice (6:5-6). There follows a section on wordiness and prolixity in prayer (6:7-8). The true spirit of prayer is illustrated by the ideal example which Jesus himself taught: the Our Father (6:9-13). To its petition for forgiveness of faults, the evangelist finally adds a saying about mutual forgiveness, which in his mind is particularly important (6:14-15).

[5]*"And when you pray, do not be like the hypocrites. For they love to pray standing around in the synagogues and at the street corners so that they catch men's eyes. Truly, I tell you: they have received their reward. [6]But when you pray, go into your room and shut the door and pray to your Father in secret; and your Father, who sees (also) what is secret, will repay you."*

In prayer man expresses his recognition of God and his submission to him. He who prays confesses God as the Lord of his life. Prayer is not really a kind of pious practice which is also part of life and must be done now and then. Prayer is man's deliberate turning of himself towards his origin. Even in this sublime act the venom of self-seeking can seep in. It is as with almsgiving. A seasoning of vanity and the desire for praise does not only reduce the value of the act. It destroys it entirely. Instead of being directed towards God, the act is diverted away and bent back on man. It is a radical perversion of the thing intended. Man is sought instead of God. It is undoubtedly no caricature when Jesus describes it as: They love to stand around in the synagogues and at the street corners in order to pray. . .

Jesus indicates a sure way which guards against self-deceit and vanity. " Go into your room and shut the door." There, where no human eye can see you, you will be able to show that you are concerned with God. Jesus does not mean that God is closer to us in our room, in our quiet, familiar retreat, than anywhere else, say in the market place, in crowds or in the gathering for public worship. God is everywhere present and should be found everywhere. What is important here is: that prayer must be free from all mixture of self-seeking. Anyone who has thus learned true prayer " in his room " will be surely able to remain in prayer outside on the streets and in the business of everyday life. He will come also to public worship with the right attitude. He has no need to be afraid that the others will interpret his piety as hypocrisy. God sees also what is secret, he knows of the right attitude and holds the reward ready for him who has not sought it.

7" When you pray, do not be wordy like the heathen. For they think that they will be answered if they use many words. 8Do not act like them! For your Father knows of what you have need before you ask him."

These are only a few words, but they are apt and well-chosen. Wordiness and long-winded speech describe the method of prayer to the heathen gods as it was then practiced. Certainly, profound and genuine prayer also exists among the heathen. But the predominant impression is still that of a monstrous flood of words. The gods are invoked not just by one, but by count-less names and titles, before the suppliant comes to what he prays for. It is not rare to find fifty such names and titles. Behind it all is what Jesus remarks briefly: they believe that they will be answered more quickly and surely the more words they use. They try to make themselves persuasive to the gods; they try to force them to pay attention, actually " to tire them out " and thus make them yield. Jesus brands this as heathen. God desires the heart and the whole man and will not let himself be bought off by a flood of pious speech.

The precept of Jesus is very simple. " Do not act like them!" The simple and gripping picture of God throws its light around you: your Father knows what you need before you ask him. He knows all and sees all, even what is secret. But not with the cold and critical eye of the philosopher or scientist or indeed with the merciless exactness of the microscope. God looks upon us with a loving paternal eye. He knows exactly what we lack. We do not need to propound our needs with a great expense of words in order to draw his attention. But on the other hand, this knowledge which God has does not render our prayer superfluous. It is left to each one to recognize his poverty before God and to pray for what is necessary—but briefly and from the heart, with honest devotion and sincere confidence. Jesus shows by an example how that is to be done, giving us what will always remain our richest and most precious prayer.

⁹" *Thus therefore shall you pray: Our Father, who is in heaven, hallowed be your name.*"

After what has gone before, we understand now more easily what the address " Our Father " means on the lips of Jesus. It means in a special way his God, the God whom Jesus proclaims. Certainly, he is also the God of Israel, the God of " Abraham, Isaac and Joseph," but all the same, he is newly revealed as Father. The Father is at once first cause and provident protector. A childlike confidence and a humble reverence is directed to him. He is the authority and still the familiar confidant; he can act sternly, but never without love.

He is distinguished from the earthly father by the addition:

" who is in heaven." To say that he dwells in heaven is a metaphor. Where would we seek such a heaven in the universe of
modern astronomy? The meaning of the metaphor is that he
is above all earthly things, beyond our visible world and in contrast to it. The world is not part of him, he is wholly other.
A childlike familiarity with the Father never loses its reverent
awe. And yet, the holy, the totally different God comes so close
to us, that we may say " Father " to him. The next phrase,
" Hallowed be your name," is to be taken in one breath with
the opening address. It is the first word which forces itself upon
the speaker, the word of praise and appreciation of his glorious
name.

[10]" *Your kingdom come; your will be done on earth as it is in
heaven.*"

Now begin the petitions, which express what is really necessary
in very few words. " Your kingdom come." That is the great
prayer of the disciple. God's kingship is to reveal itself; he must
be really Lord of the world and bring about and complete what
Jesus has begun. The petition is directed to the end, to the
consummation of the world after the great judgment. That God
should be King is the first and most pressing care of the
disciples. All our yearning is directed to this end. We must
live profoundly in God; we must have seen through the present
state of the world—for all its grandeur and beauty—in order to
pray in this way. Our faith must grow by this prayer. The
next clause refers the prayer for the kingship of God to the
present time as well. When we form the prayer that God's will
should be realized here on earth as is already the case in heaven,
then something is to happen in our own day too. We ask that

God himself may assure that his will be enforced and obeyed. We men have to comprehend the demands of this will which goes forth from God and make it one with our own will. To put it in another way: when we will what God wills, then the kingship of God is already realized here on earth. He who acts first and foremost is God, because the establishment of his kingship is his own business. But man is neither excluded, nor reduced to a passive spectator. His own forces are called upon to do God's will and so make God the Lord of his life.

[11]" *Give us this day our daily bread.*"

God knows what we need before we ask him (see 6:8). Therefore the simple prayer for sufficient bread for this day is enough. We do not ask for possessions and riches, for the fullness of earthly goods with which we could make our future secure. But what we need is the necessary, the minimum for existence, what is precisely required for our own and our family life. A look at the world around us shows how realistic and necessary this petition is since countless multitudes do not have even this absolute minimum. The disciple above all needs to make this petition, for he has dedicated himself entirely to the service of the kingship. His first care is for the things of God; thus he is confident that God will give him what is necessary for life.

[12]"*And forgive us our trespasses, as we forgive those who have trespassed against us.*"

The next clause of the prayer asks for the forgiveness of trespasses. The rather striking image really says " our money debts." This is the only place where a petition of the Our Father is linked to a condition. Jesus supposes that we have pardoned one another and have forgiven each other our mutual offences. From the teaching of Jesus the condition would be already taken for granted, and only by one who knew he had fulfilled it could such a petition be directed to God. However, now the condition is expressly laid down and it remains like a thorn in the flesh. The truth is that God does not bestow everything on us unconditionally, and he does not distribute his grace at random. He is only ready to take on the burden of the sins we have committed against him when we have done the same for one another. But then pardon really comes and we may count on it.

What is here asked of God is perhaps the greatest gift that we need in regard to our private life. For sin is the heaviest burden of our life. Our own experience shows us this. Above all man knows that he cannot alone free himself from sin. He needs a doctor to remove the ulcerous growth with gentle hands—while he is never able to pay any fee. God alone is this doctor, always ready to cleanse and heal us.

Finally, this petition also looks to the end: that we stand all our life long as debtors before God will be then confirmed once more. There we hope for the great, all-embracing mercy of God. For mercy also on our unknown sins, our unconscious involvement in guilt, the unintended scandals we have set before others, all the guilt of the tumultuous history of our ancestors and of nations. What would become of us without this hope?

[13]*"And lead us not into temptation, but deliver us from evil."*

The fourth petition is a double one. The second clause continues the first and clarifies it. We ask God not to lead us into temptation, into the danger of sin. This can hardly mean that we should be preserved from the ordinary temptations of the world in the usual sense. That would be impossible since we are living in the midst of them. Nor would it even be good for us since we are to come through temptations to give steadfast proof of ourselves. Here it is a matter of one very special temptation. It is the same as that into which Jesus was led in the desert: the temptation to apostasy, to rejection of God, which in the last resort means the lordship of Satan instead of the lordship of God. Jesus underwent this and was preserved in it. But he must pray for the apostles themselves, that they do not come into temptation in the time of conflict on Mount Olivet (26:41). Everything therefore is at stake. The prayer that we make to be spared this great temptation must be ardent and urgent. For we do not know whether we can resist or whether we are equal to the assault of the adversary. If we still are steadfast in the grace of God we shall have him to thank who has heard again and again this prayer which we have uttered so often.

" But deliver us from evil." This petition concludes the prayer and sums it up. It completes the petition for the coming of the kingship. For the reason why this kingship is not yet there, or does not make progress, is that the power of evil is working against it. And so will things remain until that power is finally broken. It is far beyond our power to free ourselves from it; God alone can do that.

Thus the prayer which begins so confidently and brightly ends on a note of gloom. Every word is weighty and every petition has its own particular necessity. We must indeed often ponder these words in our heart, and let their spirit penetrate us deeply. But we should also measure our other prayers and petitions against the Lord's prayer. We must ask ourselves whether the interests proposed by Jesus also appear in our other prayers. And we must ask ourselves whether our prayers are filled by the same breadth of spirit. We have the measure here.

[14]" *For if you forgive men their offences, then will your heavenly Father also forgive you.* [15]*But if you do not forgive men, then will your heavenly Father also not forgive your offences.*"

The same idea expressed above in the third petition is here formulated as a law. The language is that of law. The thoughts are strongly welded together, each exclusive of the other. First comes the positive, then the negative instance: if you forgive men—if you do not forgive men. Each time the action of God is made dependent on our action. There are no gaps and no exceptions. The parable of the merciless servant illustrates this saying in a striking manner (18:23–35). There are only a few words from the lips of Jesus which are so inexorably definite. No community can live a truly Christian life if it does not have this law deeply embedded in its heart so that it dominates its actions. We cannot open our mouths to approach God for forgiveness, if we ourselves are still hardened against another.

ON FASTING (6:16-18)

[16]" *But when you fast, do not put on a gloomy look like the hypocrites. For they make themselves uncomely, in order that they may appear to fast in the eyes of men. Truly, I tell you, they have received their reward.* [17]*But when you fast, anoint your head and wash your face,* [18]*that your fasting may not be seen by men, but by your Father, who is in secret; and your Father, who sees (also) what is secret, will repay you.*"

Fasting was a matter for the whole people in ancient times. The sins that were committed in Israel were not merely the individual offence committed by each person, but a guilt which lay upon the whole people. All should fast in sorrow and repentance. There were cities ready to repent which accepted the call and were converted, as did even the heathen city of Nineveh at the preaching of the prophet Jonas (see Jon. 3). The catastrophic fall of Jerusalem under the assault of the Babylonian army was a judgment upon the people who had refused to do penance. The individual could also fast privately for his own sins or as a representative for the sins of the people.

The Pharisees had a high esteem for voluntary fasting, and practiced it diligently, but hardly with the correct spirit. They wish to fast before God to show him their readiness to be converted. And what should have been done for God alone becomes a public spectacle. Everyone is to see how they afflict and crush themselves. They put on a fanatical, gloomy look, strew ashes on their heads, go around in ragged clothes—an exhibition that cannot be more ridiculous. They too, since they count on the praise of the crowd, have already received their reward and can expect no other.

Jesus does not reject fasting, not even voluntary fasting. For it can be a genuine expression of the repentant heart. But anyone who thus fasts, must " anoint his head and wash his face." People should not notice what he is doing. Outwardly he must appear perfectly normal, careful of his appearance, and with a joyous countenance. That gives a guarantee that the intention directed to God does not conflict with any intention directed towards men. What is thus hidden is seen all the same by God and given its reward, for once more it is true that he sees what is concealed; he knows the movements of the heart and the pure intention. The outward show means nothing to him.

This saying about fasting holds good for the time when Jesus, the bridegroom, has departed from us. While he is living with the disciples and doing the work of God on earth, there is a season of joy, since " the bridegroom is with them. But the days will come, when the bridegroom is taken from them, and then they will fast " (9 : 15). A new fast is then inaugurated in expectation of the return of the bridegroom. The separation is a time of sadness, but also a time of preparation, of expiation for one's own sins and all the sins of the world, a time of wakeful watching and of humble service—until the time when the marriage feast of the Lamb with his bride, the church, is really celebrated (Rev. 22:3ff). Our fasting takes on forms other than those which were customary among the Jews of those days, among the ancient Christians, and even in the Middle Ages. Our type of fasting, adapted as it is to our own day, must also be measured against Jesus' warning. Even here the danger of hypocrisy and of serving men waits for us, especially among " the pious." We can only be sure of fasting before God, when we avoid all side-glances towards our fellow men, and love to stay hidden.

The True Justice in Undivided Service of God (6:19-7:12)

The great theme of true justice is continued. The sections which we have met up to this formed an inner unity and were linked in such a way that the connection could be seen. Now we meet with a number of diverse single sayings of Jesus. They are all placed under the standpoint which we have met already: true justice must be wholly directed towards God. God is the means and the end. This must be effective in all fields of our activity and in every individual question.

ON LAYING UP TREASURES (6:19-21)

[19]*" Do not lay up for yourselves treasures on earth where the moth and the worm destroy, and where thieves break in and steal. [20]Rather lay up for yourselves treasures in heaven where neither moth nor worm destroy and where thieves do not break in and steal. [21]For where your treasure is, there your heart will also be."*

The possessive urge is part of our nature. Men's mind and efforts are directed towards acquiring, increasing and holding on to possessions. Here, however, it is not only a question of possessions but of treasures. By this is meant great and valuable possessions, large landed estates, massive houses, precious ornaments and piles of money. No matter how sure and permanently valuable all that may seem, its supposed solidity is actually quite fragile. Small animals can destroy things of considerable value. Moths eat the precious cloth of silk, worms reduce to an empty shell the chests of the finest wood. Other men become envious and hunt for ways to take possession of such goods: " Thieves break in and steal." Quickly gotten, quickly gone. Jesus soberly describes this experience which is within the reach of everyone. How futile and worthless are such efforts, how wastefully are our forces spent on highly questionable and unstable prizes.

I point out to you another goal which is worth striving for with all your might and guarantees things of permanent value: " Lay up for yourselves treasures in heaven." There the valuables are stored in security. Neither destructive insects nor treacherous thieves can make inroads upon them in heaven, that is, in God's hands. Whatever is invested in God cannot be devalued. What sort of treasure is this? In the first place, it is certainly the dedication of the heart to God. And with that it is also everything which the disciple does with the intention of truly serving God. The "good works" (5:16), the superabundant justice which goes as far as love of enemies (5:21-48), "pious practices" too—all that can become a treasure when it is done in the right spirit.

The last word is again of startling simplicity: "For where your treasure is, there your heart will also be." Jesus is conscious of this deep-seated effort after riches and valuables in which men seek happiness. The heart, the inner man, is always involved in it. If the heart clings to earthly treasures and is consumed by love of them, it is then as susceptible to destruction as earthy things. But if it has given itself to heavenly treasures and lives for them, then it has the prospect of being for ever secure with God. It sounds obvious, a logical conclusion. But how difficult it is to think and act as the saying demands!

THE LIGHT OF THE EYE (6:22-23)

²²" The light of the body is the eye. If therefore your eye is healthy your whole body will be full of light. ²³But if your eye is unwell, your whole body will be dark. If then the light that is in you is darkness, how great will the darkness be!"

Jesus starts once more from a fact of experience: the healthy or diseased (even blind) eye makes the whole body bright or dark. But neither expression is clear-cut: the healthy is also the good eye (of the heart), the diseased the evil eye. The bodily eye is a metaphor for the heart. We are to think of both at the same time. The whole man is mirrored in the eye, his thinking and feeling, the purity or the corruption of his life. The eye is the light of the body, the infallible mirror of the soul. If this light is clear and bright, so too is the whole man. If however the eye is evil, corrupt and wicked, if it looks slyly and lustfully at the world, then the whole body and the man is in darkness. This saying is in the nature of a parable, and needs to be interpreted. Jesus gives the solution in the last phrase: " If then the light that is in you is darkness, how great will the darkness be!" What does this mean? The heart is to be directed entirely to God, it must live among the treasures in heaven. Then the whole man will be well. If the heart has spent itself on earthly goods, it has become spiritually blind, and the whole man is in darkness. He does not see the true good, and he gropes in the dark. But God is the light. He makes man full of light, and he should shine out of man's eyes.

TRUE SERVICE OF GOD (6:24)

24" No man can serve two masters. For either he will hate the one and love the other, or he will cling to the one and despise the other. You cannot serve God and Mammon."

The contrast is expressed again and again in new forms, and the disciple is called again and again to the same decision: treasures on earth—treasures in heaven, darkness—light, Mammon—God. Here too a natural experience leads to the spiritual region. Each one can serve only one master with all his might. In the fullest sense, however, this is true only with regard to God, who does indeed demand the whole man and can tolerate no compromise. Only with regard to God is the Either-Or valid in the full sense; he knows only one thing matters for our salvation—himself alone.

Everywhere that God's right as lord and master is challenged, the evil one is concealed. He is master of manifold forms of contradiction and enmity. He is particularly deceptive when he disguises himself with the mask of Mammon. In itself that is only earthly goods, the piling up of possessions, of all sorts of riches. But we also know from experience about the glistening power of gold and the bewitching splendour of earthly valuables. For Jesus, riches are always " unjust," an almost demonic power which takes the heart in thrall and holds it fettered. He who falls into the hands of Mammon, falls into the hands of the devil. There is only one whom man can truly serve: God, who is the light of our life, in whose hands the true treasures and our heart are safely preserved.

ON ANXIETY (6:25-34)

25" *Therefore I tell you: be not anxious about your life, what you shall eat, nor about your body, what you shall put on. Is not life more than food, and the body more than clothing?"*

He who lives entirely for God, as the three preceding sayings have explained, will be no longer impelled by anxiety about his earthly life. In the long passage which follows there is only one theme: to demonstrate how superfluous is anxiety about earthly things in view of the great Father. This anxiety is concerned above all with two fundamental human needs: food for maintaining life, and clothes for protecting the body. The effort to gain food and clothing is not lightly dismissed. Jesus speaks of an anxiety which is misdirected, that is, feverish efforts and craven keenness, which tend to exclude God. Both rich and poor can be the victims of such anxiety.

Jesus makes a general statement to begin with: " Is not life more than food, and the body more than clothing?" Since God has made you a gift of the more precious things, life and body, will he not also take care of the less precious? We get the impression from many men, that the whole meaning of their life is completely expressed in obtaining such goods. They believe that their happiness lies in assuring themselves sustenance and in satisfying that need. And at the same time they forget that it is precisely not " from bread alone " that we live.

26Consider the birds in the sky: they neither sow nor reap nor gather into barns, and yet your heavenly Father nourishes them. Are you not worth much more than they? 27But which of you by being anxious can add even a cubit to his length of life?

Here Jesus speaks of the first subject—anxiety about food. There is a delightful example from nature in which the guiding hand of the Father can be seen. For one to whom God is everywhere present, and visibly at work, the feeding of the birds is not just a natural process, but a miracle of fatherly providence. They make no efforts to build storehouses for the future. They live from day to day: " Your heavenly Father nourishes them." If that is true of such tiny creatures, how much more with regard to men, whose life is infinitely more precious, and much closer to the heart of the Father? God knows in fact what we need before we ask him for it (see 6:8). He watches over us constantly and takes care of the outcome. To think in other terms is also quite futile since, in any case, he has fixed the length of our life. No matter how much pains a man takes and no matter how busy and active he is—he cannot lengthen his life.

We must pay attention only to what is meant and silence the questions that arise: what about animals that do lay up stores of food and provide for the future? What matters is to be in accord with God's plan, and not with mere earthly advantage. How often have we experienced the truth of these words in our own life? Are they not also effective in times of prosperity and security?

²⁸"*And why are you anxious about clothing? Consider the lilies of the fields, how they grow; they neither work nor spin.* ²⁹*But I tell you: not even Solomon in all his glory was clothed like one of these.* ³⁰*But if God so clothes the grass of the fields, which grows today and tomorrow is cast into the oven, how much more you, you men of little faith!*"

Now comes the second subject—anxiety about clothing. Jesus once more turns the gaze of his disciples towards nature, the glorious garden of God. Even unremarkable plants like the lilies of the field mentioned here have been given a great beauty by God. Not only are the roses or the magnificent dahlias clothed in beauty, but even the wild flowers which grow among the grass. That paragon of splendour and palatial enjoyment, King Solomon, is only a trifle compared with this simple beauty. It passes quickly and is burnt along with the grass. Although God has decked it out so magnificently, will not the same Father who lavishes so much care on the flowers also take care of you, so that you will be able to dress yourselves properly? You must have faith and trust that God really cares about such things. Do not be men of little faith, who exercise their confidence only sparingly and begrudge its use, who trust too little in God and continually burden him with their own timorousness.

³¹"*Do not therefore be anxious, asking yourselves: what shall we*

eat? or: what shall we drink? or: how shall we be clothed?
³²For after all these things do the heathen seek. But our heavenly
Father knows that you have need of all this. ³³But seek first the
kingdom and its justice, and all these things will be given to you
in addition."

These words sum up what has been said. First, the timorous
" men of little faith " are always wondering: what shall we have
to eat and drink and wear? He who asks such questions, he who
looks only to his own effort to give him security in life, is acting
like the heathen. They know nothing of God and his fatherly
providence and are therefore entirely dependent on their own
resources. But you know God, he is " your heavenly Father."
When you really believe that, then you also know that he knows
all your needs.

It now becomes perfectly clear that Jesus is not trying at all to
prevent us working for our earthly existence. He only points out
the main thing in the life of the disciple: " Seek first the kingdom of God." Here this means in practice: seek God himself
before all other things. He who strives for the kingship of God
commits himself entirely to the glorious majesty and the fatherly
kindness of God. But then is added: " and its justice." It is the
same justice that we have come up against several times already,
that very justice which God looks for in us and with which we
are to respond to him. It is the perfection of the heavenly Father,
which is to find its expression in us: the justice which makes us
fit for the kingship—now at this very moment, and above all at
the end. And this tells us that it is not a matter of our own
achievements, but of being penetrated, transformed, and enkindled by God and his will. That must be our desire, our mind,
and our search—our own work finds expression only in this.

Then not only will our cares be lightened with regard to our bodily needs, but God will give of his own accord all that is necessary. He who is filled by the one effort which is important will have no more ambitions for himself. He goes on working of course, he earns money, he makes purchases. But this is a service which he performs in God. His heart does not live in such things in the last resort. We should have the courage to take this risk. Great saints like Francis of Assisi and John Bosco have shown us by their own experience that we can take God at his word.

" Be not therefore anxious about tomorrow; for tomorrow will take care of itself. Sufficient for each day is its own trouble."

This clause comes at the end like an epilogue, a modest finale for the important discourse. It is not theology, but a piece of home-spun wisdom. Every day brings as a matter of course a certain amount of toil and trouble. We must not make the amount still larger by anxiety about tomorrow! In spite of its simplicity the saying shows that we still have our feet on the solid earth. To give up all anxious care does not mean, in the mind of Jesus, that we are absolved from daily work, that we escape the countless self-same duties, the monotony of the daily routine which is often so tiresome. All that remains as it is. What is new is the attitude of the disciple: his innermost effort is not tied to such things but directed towards God. Then all our little efforts become easy, and are lit up by the light from on high.

ON JUDGING (7:1-5)

¹*" Judge not, that you be not judged. ²For with the judgment*

*whereby you judge, you shall be judged, and with the measure
wherewith you measure, it will be measured out to you."*

Our distorted nature is inclined to pass judgment on others. And
this judgment easily turns into one of condemnation. This is
what Jesus means when he forbids us to judge our fellow men.
The reason for this is that we ourselves be not judged, that is,
particularly strongly condemned. He who judges another arro-
gates to himself a right which he does not possess at all. He pre-
sumes to exercise a right which belongs to God, from whom
alone a correct verdict is possible and legitimate. The man who
judges has gone beyond the measure allotted to man, and is now
sent back to his proper bounds. Thereby we are also told that
every human verdict of condemnation is provisional and uncertain, that it never does full justice to the case. It is better to
be ten times silent than once unjust. When speaking of forgiveness, Jesus had already made our conduct towards each other the
norm or measure of God's conduct towards us. Only he who
forgives the other may also count on God's forgiveness (6:
12.14f.). Here this principle is applied to our judgments. The
same sentence which we pass on our brothers will be pronounced
on us by God. God will measure us according to the same rule
that we apply to our brothers. He who expects consideration and
mercy and a magnanimous verdict from God must himself have
accorded it to his fellow men. He who judges sharply and coldly,
unjustly and above all slanderously, must reckon with the fact
that God will treat him unmercifully too.

*³" Why do you see the mote in the eye of your brother, but do not
notice the plank in your own eye? ⁴Or why do you say to your
brother: ' Let me remove the mote from your eye;' and behold,*

the plank is sticking to your own eye? *⁵Hypocrite! First remove the plank from your own eye, and then you will be able to see how to remove the mote from the eye of your brother."*

A dramatic example! He who condemns another is himself ripe for condemnation since we are all debtors with regard to God. This matter of passing judgment is linked up with criticizing and trying to correct the faults of others. In doing this, we often fail to remark our own weaknesses and view those of others with a magnifying glass. Look at yourself first, says Jesus, and improve your own way of life. When you have succeeded in doing that, you may then come to the aid of your brother. If you act otherwise, you are a hypocrite, who appears, or tries to appear, better than he really is.

The hint given here about the brotherly duty of mutual correction becomes a clear statement later in the Gospel (18 : 15–20). All that follows here is that the right of blaming a brother is reserved to him who has first examined and improved himself. That is the way things should be among Christians. Has that penetrated the marrow of our bones?

ON THAT WHICH IS HOLY (7:6)

⁶" Do not give what is holy to the dogs, and do not cast your pearls before swine, so that they do not trample them under their feet, and turn against you and rend you."

The background of this saying is not very clear. It is a directive for the missionary work of the disciples. The pearl is the gospel, the word of God. It may only be proclaimed where it is readily accepted. It must not be thrown away and wasted. It must be dispensed carefully. Otherwise, not only will something holy be desecrated, trampled by swine, but the messenger himself will be endangered. The preaching has called forth rejection of the message. And that rejection will grow into hatred of the preachers. The hearers turn and rend them.

Jesus had undoubtedly announced that his disciples would meet with failure and even persecution. But that must not be brought about by their own imprudence and lack of ability to size up a situation. Much sectarian importunity in the spreading of the gospel is condemned by this directive of the Lord. We must show charity toward all men—but with regard to the word, the essence of the message, the divine mystery itself, we must be tactful and careful. The disciples must keep both things before their minds: the urgency of proclaiming the gospel— and the duty of not letting the holy word be profaned and blasphemed. This is also an important warning for us, since we live among people to whom in many cases the Christian message has become utterly foreign.

On Prayer of Petition (7:7-11)

[7]" *Ask, and you shall receive; seek, and you shall find; knock, and it will be opened unto you.* [8]*For everyone who asks receives, and he who seeks will find, and to him who knocks it will be opened.*"

Since God is the Father, who knows all about us and concerns himself with everything, he will always be there for us. The prayer of petition shows whether we really believe. In such prayer we have to confess that we are dependent upon him and cannot succeed alone. Prayer of petition, rightly made, is a touchstone of our faith and of our humility. "Ask, and you shall receive "—that sounds like a law. Prompt answer follows upon the confident proposal of our needs. No distinction is made here between what is important and unimportant, what is justifiable and unjustifiable in our requests. That is treated of in other texts. Here it is a matter of the certainty that God hears us.

He who has understood what has gone before, and lives accordingly, will experience every day how simple that is. He whose heart is set upon God and who lives for God always makes his prayer " in God." He knows with certainty that all the petitions that he thus makes " in God " are heard at the very moment he speaks. This is the secret of the prayer of petition to which Jesus so often attributes the certainty of being heard. It is not a means of putting pressure on God, but the way of life for the disciple who places himself entirely under God's kingship. It will be quite natural for him.

⁹" Or is there any of you who will give his son a stone when he asks him for bread? ¹⁰Or who will give him a serpent when he asks for fish? ¹¹If therefore you who are evil know how to give good gifts to your children, how much more will your Father in heaven give good gifts to those who ask!"

We have only to believe that God is Father. Then everything follows at once. It is the same as in your own life. After all, you are not the cruel step-mother who gives the children a stone instead of bread, or a serpent instead of fish. You look after your children and your families; you make it a point of honor to nourish and gladden them. You know exactly what are the duties of a good father. That is how God deals with us. With only one difference—the best that can be said of earthly fathers is far truer of him because " you are evil." The word sounds bitter. Jesus did not propound a doctrine on the nature of man, not even here in the Sermon on the Mount. But now and again a gleam of light falls on the picture of man whom he has in mind. Such is the case here. He knows what is in man and he knows that man is wedded to evil. What Jesus means here is not so much the fact that we act wickedly time after time, but rather this general proximity, this kinship, this inclination to sin. It is so strong and has got its teeth so deeply into us that it makes us " evil "—if only in nothing but sin and lie.

In any case, we give good things to our children and keep them safe from harm. God does that far better than any earthly father. The one and only thing he thinks of is how he can distribute good things. If we ask for something, we need never be afraid that we will be given something harmful, not even when the " good things " come to us in the form of purifying sickness, loneliness, persecution, or whatever form of suffering that may arrive. It comes from the Father; it is always good for us.

The " Golden Rule " (7:12)

[12]" *Everything therefore that you wish that men should do to you, do also to them; for that is the law and the prophets."*

This rule for human relationships is not typically Christian. Noble heathens and Jews have also laid down the same principles : we ourselves must treat others in the same way we wish to be treated. Jesus also pronounces this word of natural insight and worldly wisdom. But it has a new meaning on his lips. For the measure which he lays down is different from what it could be with heathens and Jews. Jesus has spoken of a love which knows no measure because it takes its measure from God and does not exclude even the enemy. What I am to expect from my brother, my fellow Christian, and what he may expect from me is this sort of love. The golden rule is only a framework; it can be filled with various contents. Of course, no one will insist on his right to this manner of treatment. He will always make this demand on himself first of all. However, the sense of what either pains or rejoices me, will be a sure guide for how I am to act towards another.

The Disciple in face of Judgment (7:13-27)

In the last section (6:19–7:12), the structure of the Sermon on the Mount had already appeared in a looser fashion. So it remains to the end. But the last items are collected according to one viewpoint: the expectation of the end, the prospect of judgment. First comes the call to enter by the "narrow gate" (7:13f.). Then comes a warning against false prophets, which can only be understood easily if seen in the light of the end (7:15–20). After this is a section which speaks of the true criterion of the disciple at judgment (7:21–23). The whole discourse ends with the powerful parable of the building of the house (7:24–27).

LIFE OR LOSS (7:13-14)

[13]" *Enter in by the narrow gate; for wide is the gate and broad the way which leads to destruction, and many are they that enter thereby.* [14]*For narrow is the gate and strait the way which leads to life, and few they are that find it.*"

The metaphor of the two ways is an ancient one. It is often used in the Psalms to describe the way, that is, the way of life of the wicked and the just, and to distinguish them. Here again images are taken together: the gate, which can be narrow or broad, and the way, which can be spacious or restricted. Both images say something valid. The way is an image of the course of life; the latter is in the flux of time and is a restless wandering until it reaches a certain boundary. This boundary is described by the second image—the gate. It describes a triple event: death, judgment, a new start after a break. These two pictures combine to make the meaning of our life clear.

Jesus uses them here in a grim and even pessimistic saying. The one possibility offered by the broad, roomy gate and the easy, comfortable way is destruction; the other possibility offered by the narrow gate and the painfully restricted way is life. One means loss, the horror of hell; the other salvation, the glory of redemption. By " life " something perfect is meant; the whole man, body and soul, being rendered happy by God for all eternity. There is no third possibility.

The most terrifying thing, however, is the numerical proportion. Many go through the wide gate to destruction, and few they are who find the narrow gate. Here we touch upon one of the most agonizing riddles of human life, the question of election. "Are there few that shall be saved?" (Lk. 13:23). Who will be saved and who not? Has God predestined them beforehand, and how efficaciously?

The word here says something primarily about the present, something of this kind: the easy path of mediocrity, the way of sin and blasphemy, is well trodden. While the narrow way, which is sharp and steep in the direction of God, the way of the Sermon on the Mount, finds few followers. This was Jesus' own experience, and that of the primitive Church after him. Our own knowledge seems to teach us the same thing. But then all the emphasis is on the summons at the beginning: " Enter in by the narrow gate!" This means: Take pains to find the right way and the right gate. It is not your business to speculate about how many will be saved or not. Your business is to find the entrance that leads to life.

WARNING AGAINST FALSE PROPHETS (7:15-20)

[15]" *Beware of false prophets who come to you in sheep's clothing, but are ravening wolves within.*"

Often in the Old Testament God had to warn against false prophets who were not called by him and did not proclaim his word. If the devil imitates God, it is not surprising that he can invent a caricature that can compete with all that is holy. It remained so in the early church as well. There we find apostles and false apostles, teachers and teachers of heresy, prophets and pseudo-prophets. It is not easy to recognize them. For they wear the cloak of correct doctrine with an ostensible lack of self-interest. By sheep's clothing we must no doubt understand what is precisely Christian, the appearance of Christian faith and life. The outward impression completely contradicts the inner nature: in reality they are ravenous wolves. The wolf is the natural enemy of the flock and he mixes with the sheep unrecognized in his disguise. He abuses their innocent trust, to show his teeth suddenly and tear the sheep in pieces. That is what will happen to those who seek themselves instead of God.

The disciples are in danger, not only from without by means

of persecution and malicious tongues (5:11f.), but also from within through false prophets. This danger from within is hard to recognize; it is not easy to distinguish the true from the false doctrine. Here we are given a means of discernment which is unassailable. The words of the false prophets do not count so much; in matters of preaching, discourse, and lectures one can be deceived. But there is never any deception when one considers their fruits.

[16]" *By their fruits can you know them. Does anyone gather grapes from thorns or figs from thistles?* [17]*So every good tree bears good fruit, but the evil tree bears evil fruit.* [18]*A good tree cannot bear evil fruit, nor can an evil tree bear good fruit.*"

Jesus shows the way by appealing to the course of nature. There we have the law that what is strong and healthy bears healthy fruit, whereas the weak and sickly produces worthless fruit. The same is true of man. His life forms a unity: his dispositions, his thoughts, his actions and his will must be in harmony. If a rift develops in this unity, if for instance a man carries out a commandment of God only outwardly and formally while deep within himself he thinks otherwise, this rift will also become recognizable outwardly. Only what is whole can maintain itself in the long run. The fruit are not individual acts, but, as with the tree, all the fruit together, the whole life of the man.

[19]" *Every tree that does not bear good fruit, will be cut down and cast into the fire.* [20]*Therefore: by their fruits shall you know them.*"

The verdict of history is the verdict of God—this saying is valid to a certain extent even here. Much that has no power of survival in time and in earthly life will not be saved even here from the menace of judgment. It is already judged here on earth, so that the final verdict only confirms the first. The rotten and hollow tree which has produced no nourishing fruit is good for nothing. The farmer cuts it down and burns it. This image had already been used by John the Baptist to describe the judgment. So too Jesus: the barren tree is delivered over to the judgment of God and destroyed in its fire. This applies here to the false prophets above all. But it is also true for the other disciples of Jesus. What has been unceasingly inculcated in all the preceding sections now receives new sharpness and urgency in the face of judgment. Only what is whole, a life fully mature in faith and love, can abide the fire of judgment.

PROFESSION OF FAITH AND DEEDS AT JUDGMENT (7:21-23)

[21]*" Not everyone who says to me, ' Lord, Lord,' will enter the kingdom of heaven, but he who does the will of my Father in heaven."*

Deeds, not words, really matter: not even the words of profession of faith and of praise. " Lord—*Kyrie*," is the primordial invocation of Jesus in which faith in his exaltation found its powerful expression. Jesus was invoked as " *Kyrie* " in the liturgy, as is still done today in the " Lord Have Mercy." But this confession of the lips to Jesus as Lord must correspond to confession in deeds. And the works must be directed to nothing but " the will of my Father in heaven." Here we have the unity of the old and new covenant: the will of God—proclaimed in the old covenant and " fulfilled " by Jesus—and the acknowledgement of Jesus as Lord. Jesus maintained no special doctrinal position; the Christian teacher and prophet may not do so either. The will of God is the end which points out the way to all. This declaration could be a bridge to Christ for the Jews.

[22]" *Many will say to me on that day: 'Lord, Lord, have we not prophesied in your name, and in your name driven out spirits and in your name performed many wonders?'* [23]*But then I will say to them: 'I never knew you; depart from me, you doers of evil.'* "

On the day of judgment those who appear before Jesus know that he is judge and that he has to pass sentence. They turn to him and invoke him as they once did in the liturgy with " Lord, have mercy; Lord, have mercy." Then they begin to recount, not only the sermons and doctrines they have pronounced, the letters and books they have written, but their works. These works testify to a special endowment with supernatural powers. Jesus had first equipped the apostles with them: " Heal the sick, waken the dead, cleanse the lepers, drive out spirits " (Mt. 10 : 7). They also performed the same deeds later in their missionary work. Others were endowed with gifts of speech and wonders wrought by the Spirit. They say: we have prophesied, that is, spoken prophetically in the Spirit to build up the church—we have exorcized spirits—we have worked miracles. And all that " in your name," that is, appealing to the might of the Lord and invoking his name, as we see from the healings done by Peter: " In the name of Jesus Christ of Nazareth, stand up and walk!" (Acts 3 : 6). They were works which were performed out of faith in Jesus and in the service of the church. But they stand alone and isolated beside their own lives. They themselves have not done the will of God.

The sentence of the judge is extraordinarily sharp: " I never knew you." The messenger of Jesus should perform only the work of the Lord; he must be the hand and the arm of the exalted Lord. This is what is always meant when the apostles say: in his name, or, in the name of Jesus. Just as Christ is in the office, so he must also be in the personal life of the messenger. Christ recognizes him who is wholly at one with him. Christ is in him and with him because he guides his thoughts and directs his paths. It is a loving recognition, mutual familiarity and cooperation. But if a split runs through this life, then not only does one of two engines cease to function, but the other has no effect. No displays, no matter how brilliant and wonderful, can ever replace the want of a love active in work. If this is missing, even charismatic gifts remain hollow and empty.

In their earthly life the office bearers have not made themselves fully one with the *Kyrios* but have denied him certain regions. There has been a failure of moral steadfastness. Because they have separated themselves partially from Jesus, he now separates himself totally from them: " Depart from me, you doers of evil." The words come from Psalm 6:9. Here they become the verdict of judgment which brings them separation from the *Kyrios*, and so from life. When he turns away, only death remains behind.

THE TWO HOUSES (7:24-27)

²⁴" *Everyone therefore who hears these my words and does them shall be like a prudent man who built his house upon a rock.* ²⁵*And the rain fell, the floods came, and the storms blew and hurled themselves against that house, but it did not collapse; for it was founded upon rock.* ²⁶*And everyone who hears these my*

*words and does them not shall be like a foolish man who built
his house upon sand.* [27]*And the rain fell, the floods came, and
the storms blew and hurled themselves against that house, and it
collapsed, and its fall was great."*

This is a parable of tremendous impact. With bold strokes Jesus
draws two pictures: the house that a prudent man built upon
rock—and the house of a foolish man who used sand for his
foundation. One must imagine for a moment the landscape
and the way of building houses in Palestine. The house is loosely
put together of stones, mud, and wood. The rain mostly comes
suddenly and heavily and rushes in streams over the rocky
ground, since there is no forest land or pasture to absorb the
water. A house with rock foundation is not washed away: the
flood water streams by to left and right of it, but cannot under-
mine the foundation. The other house starts to totter as the
sand starts to flow away with the flood water and undermines
the shaking house from below.

Jesus says: He who hears these my words and follows them
shall be like a prudent man, namely, on the day of judgment.
The tempest is described in such harsh colors that one is reminded of that tremendous catastrophe which will bring history
to a close: the rain poured down, the streams came, the storms
blew and hurled themselves against that house. The picture gives
a warning of the terrible tempest of the last days. It is then
decided definitively what happens to the house. No one can
begin to build again a second time. If the house has collapsed,
it lies for ever in ruins. These words lend a sense of urgency
to the whole discourse. You can build only one house. The
words of Jesus show where the foundation is to be laid if you
are to survive the storming gales of judgment. But hearing

and knowing this is not enough if you do not really build on a rock foundation, that is, unless you do according to these words and your knowledge. Everything that has been said up to this is urgent, not merely because God wills it so and because it has been revealed by Jesus, but because the time is short for everyone. There is only one life; it cannot be repeated. At the end stands the inexorable judgment. Only he can sustain it, whose life has been built with one single end in view: God—God's kingship—and his justice.

The Conclusion (7:28-29)

[28]*And it came to pass when Jesus had finished these words that the crowds were awe-struck at his doctrine.* [29]*For he taught like one having authority and not like the scribes.*

Jesus' first great discourse is ended. It is the most condensed summary of his message. Matthew has put it at the beginning and also made it the foundation of his gospel. Everything that follows is to be seen in its light.

Men "were awe-struck at his doctrine." This is not being terrified by something sensational, holding one's breath at the bold daring of a tight-rope dance, trembling anxiously at danger or the nearness of death. It is the fear of God which penetrates the very marrow; it is being gripped by holiness and supernatural power. This happens when the very center of one's life is touched, when the deepest levels of the soul are stirred by God. We tremble before news from the other world, at the claim that is made upon our heart. This terror is necessary and healthy.

And now comes the reason for this: " For he taught like one having authority." The usual manner of instruction falls short of this. The scribes hand on and expound the will of God. They are indeed authorized servants of the faith. The technique of their instruction consists in taking a saying of scripture and citing the opinions of the learned about it, whereby they themselves maintain one of these opinions. The only word which is uttered and which works in the spirit and with force is the word of scripture. All the rest is application and exposition and therefore human word. But here someone speaks " with authority." He does not cite the rabbis and their opinions, but he himself declares independently what the will of God is. Like a divine lawgiver he even sets his own word above the word of the law. " But I tell you . . ."—no one can speak like this unless he comes immediately from God with a direct divine mandate. His teaching fulfills " the law and the prophets." The word of Jesus comes to us also with the same majesty and authority. Whether we read it or hear it or meditate it in common: he himself addresses us " with authority."

What leaves the people so deeply terror-struck is something more than the authority with which he speaks. For this authority expresses itself in the personal summons—a claim which one cannot avoid; a demand which calls for the transformation of the heart; the manifestation of Spirit and force which supports this claim. Here a word of a unique nature has been uttered, a " new teaching " indeed, but a doctrine with challenging force. One cannot remain neutral in face of this word. There are only two ways here: either to remain closed in on oneself, or to be thrown open to God. And that means conversion, faith, a new life.

The Deeds of the Messiah (8:1—9:34)

The work follows upon the word. Jesus proclaims the kingdom of God both in his spoken message and in the deeds which manifest him as the saviour. Both go together and complement one another. Matthew has undoubtedly put the following sections together from this viewpoint. Miracles alternate with controversies. Three sections can be distinguished rather clearly (8:1-17; 8:18—9:13; 9:14-34).

First Cycle of Miracles (8:1-17)

THE HEALING OF THE LEPER (8:1-4)

The event takes place in front of the great crowd of people who have just heard Jesus' discourse. They are all to experience now his preaching as it appears in his work.

¹As he came down from the mountain a great multitude followed him. ²And behold, a leper came up to him, fell down before him and said: " Lord, if you wish, you can make me clean."

Leprosy is a scourge which has not been totally overcome even today. Men in that lamentable condition had to go through a long sickness in which they saw one limb after another dying off until they themselves quietly passed away. In addition, they were outcasts in Israel. In the shape of leprosy they were bearing sin on their body—as the rabbis taught—and were allowed partnership neither in divine worship nor in social life. They had to warn people of their approach from a distance and no one could touch them or give them shelter. Anything they touched also became unclean at once. They lived as prisoners of a jealously guarded taboo.

The leper addresses Jesus with the majestic name of " Lord." And he who has just spoken as the majestic lawgiver is now moved to a majestic deed. The confidence of the leper is boundless: " If you wish, you can make me clean." The sick man believes in the power of Jesus to conquer sickness. Whether or not he works a miracle on the leper depends solely on his will. Thus the leper puts himself completely at the disposition of the other, and leaves himself to the free will of God. Jesus had already taught men to pray in this way (see 7:7–11).

3He stretched out his hand, touched him, and said: " It is my will, be cleansed." And his leprosy was cleansed immediately.

Jesus answers him in the same terms: " It is my will, be cleansed." In saying this he proclaims two things: that he really can do what is attributed to him and that he also wishes to do it. It is his gracious and merciful will which pours itself out upon every unhappy creature, not the self-centered will of one who wishes to display his own greatness. The gesture (" he stretched out his hand and touched him ") underlines the word. He is not afraid of becoming unclean himself or of being charged by his enemies with transgressing the law. His outstretched hand is the lordly gesture of the conqueror. His touch brings back the poor outcast into the community of men.

4And Jesus said to him: " See to it that you tell nobody, but go and show yourself to the priests and offer the sacrifice which Moses has prescribed, in testimony to them."

Jesus commands him not to trumpet the miracle abroad, but to perform what the law prescribes silently and obediently. Jesus, who apparently has just broken the law with sovereign freedom, now directs that the law be followed out exactly. The leper's appearance before the priests is to demonstrate the completeness of the cure; the sacrifice is to be an expression of his gratitude to God, the author of the cure and the giver of new life. At the same time, it serves as testimony to the officials that nothing unlawful has taken place. Jesus is not self-seeking. He does good simply and turns the thanksgiving towards God.

Here too is verified what the programmatic sentence about " the fulfillment of the law and the prophets " said: the law is not to be abolished. But it is fulfilled by Jesus and fulfilled most radically where it is no longer necessary at all, where the sickness which the law envisaged has disappeared, where a sound and healthy life has been given back by God instead of the deteriorated forms of life which the law was to regulate. Here comes the kingship of God, here it becomes Event. And men's eyes are directed to the future in all its fullness—when wholeness of life will be granted for all and law will be no longer necessary.

The Heathen Centurion (8:5–13)

Jesus worked the previous miracle on an Israelite, the next on a heathen. It is a sort of program: the salvation of God must reach Israel, but it must reach the heathen as well. They too are embraced by God's mercy and share in the gifts of the messianic age. We can see at the same time the order of things which God has laid down for his way of salvation: first the Jews, then the heathen. For " salvation is of the Jews." In Matthew the miracle itself does not stand out strongly. The main emphasis is on the conversation between Jesus and the centurion. It deals first with the major event of universal import which now takes place in the history of salvation, and only then with the miracle and the salvation which reveals itself at work in it.

⁵As he was going in towards Capernaum, a centurion approached him, imploring him ⁶and saying: " Lord, my servant lies paralyzed at home and suffers terrible pain." ⁷He said to him: " Should I come and heal him?" ⁸The centurion answered: " Lord, I am not worthy that you should enter under my roof; but say only one word, and my servant will be healed."

The man who approaches Jesus boldly and puts his request before him, is a heathen officer of Herod Antipas. He describes with reserve the lamentable state of his servant without asking at the start for Jesus to take action. Jesus understands him at once and asks: " Should I come and heal him?" The answer of the heathen shows the same reserve as before. He has no desire to impose upon the Jew and make him unclean by bringing him into his house. And so he disguises his courtesy under the cloak of his personal modesty: " I am not worthy that you should enter under my roof." But he trusts that Jesus can perform the cure without appearing in person. It will be enough if he utters one single word of command.

⁹" For I too am a man who must submit to authority, and I also have soldiers under me. If I say to this one, ' Go,' then he goes, and if I say to another ' Come ' then he comes, and if I say to my servant, ' Do that,' then he does it."

He thinks of Jesus as a supreme commander to whom the hostile powers of sickness must be obedient—just as he himself is subject to authority and must carry out the commands of his superior officers, and just as he himself possesses power to command, and his soldiers obey at his word. There too all that is ever required is a word which is enough to express the will of the commanding officer and secure its execution. He has not to be there in person. The commands of " Come " and " Go " also work at a distance. The discipline and the effectiveness of the troops are based on this obedience. Jesus too, with a single word of command, must be able to break the power of sickness. This is an imposing picture of Jesus which the heathen has composed for himself.

[10] *When Jesus heard this, he was amazed and said to those who were following him: " Truly, I tell you, I have found such faith in no one in Israel."*

Jesus is astonished at the words of the centurion. " He was amazed "—impressed by the greatness of the speaker. Before answering him he addresses to his companions, his brothers out of Judaism, a grave word: " I have found such faith in no one in Israel." The narrative supposes that Jesus has already been at work for some time and has found little response among his fellow countrymen. At least he did not encounter what the heathen attests here: that great and worthy picture which he has of Jesus and such unlimited confidence in his power. The two together, the picture of him and the confidence in him, Jesus calls " faith." Someone can have a lofty picture of Jesus and still have little confidence in him in a particular situation. And another can put an urgent, covetous violence into his prayer without having an enlightened picture of Jesus.

[11] *" But I tell you: Many shall come from the East and the West*

and sit down at table with Abraham and Isaac and Jacob in the
kingdom of God. ¹²*But the children of the kingdom shall be cast*
out into the outer darkness where there shall be howling and
gnashing of teeth."

That Israel does not attain to such faith and will therefore be
condemned is already prophetically proclaimed in these words.
The Jews were accustomed to picture the happiness of supernatural life in vivid images. One of these was sharing the table
of the fathers of the people of God, Abraham, Isaac and Jacob.
Since they were the descendants of Abraham, they believed that
they must also belong to his family at the fulfillment of all
things. Such confidence in physical descent from Abraham had
already been shattered by the Baptist: " From these stones
here, God can raise up children to Abraham " (3:9). Jesus goes
a step further. The true children of Abraham will be those who
possess a faith such as that of the heathen centurion. From East
and West shall they come. This was what the prophets had con-
templated: the pilgrimage of the peoples in the last days. They
are on their way and are seeking the salvation of God. The
supreme promise of participation in the kingship of God will be
fulfilled in them. Haven't many peoples of the earth already
started on this pilgrimage, driven by their yearning for peace
and salvation?

   " The children of the kingdom " —these are the children of
Israel according to the flesh. Strictly speaking they are the
natural-born heirs who await with certainty the inheritance of
the kingdom. And it is precisely these who are deprived of
fellowship at table with the patriarchs. The image which Jesus
uses for their rejection is terrifyingly grim. Just as dirty, ragged
guests are ordered to leave the diningroom, so shall they be

" cast out " into a fathomless darkness where no gleam from the festive lights of the hall can penetrate. There they gather together in a mournful cry of woe. There too they give vent to their impotent rage at being excluded from the meal and the festivities—gnashing their teeth.

13And Jesus said to the centurion: " Go; as you have believed, so shall it be done unto you." And the servant was healed at the same moment.

One thing is made clear again. No one can ever put forward a claim to salvation which is derived from tradition, the merits of his forefathers, or the mere fact of belonging to a family, an association, or a nation. The decisive thing is " such faith." He who has it will be granted what he asks for superabundantly, and still more will be bestowed, which our constantly failing courage often dares not ask for.

FURTHER HEALINGS (8:14–17)

14And Jesus entered Peter's house and saw his mother-in-law lying there sick of a fever. 15He touched her hand and the fever left her. And she stood up and served them with food.

Peter and his brother Andrew lived in Capernaum, no doubt in the little house of his parents-in-law. A serious fever felled Peter's mother-in-law. Jesus comes visiting, and heals her at once, easily and almost incidentally. He grasps her hand and the healing power streams into her and makes her instantly well. She is able to get up at once and serve the guests without difficulty. Life radiates from him.

It is a miracle told in a low key and without any flourishes. But a breath of homely warmth flows through the brief narrative. Peter belongs to him and his house offers him refreshing repose. Jesus shares their simple life and bestows on the relative of one of his disciples, as on all others, his merciful gifts.

¹⁶When it was evening they brought to him many that were possessed; and he drove out the evil spirits with a word and healed all the sick.

First the evangelist rounds off the narrative of the miracles with a word which sums up the situation (as he had already done in 4:23-25): all those possessed by demons and suffering from illness are healed as soon as they are brought to Jesus. It took place in the evening of the same day that Jesus was Peter's guest. So we may imagine that a crowd thronged together in front of the house. The sick are carried there from all the houses in the locality. For the spirits, a single word is enough to make them flee—the word of command in which the centurion had such lively faith (8:8). Jesus needs no extended exorcisms and techniques; his word suffices.

But is it not great faith that brings the people thronging to Jesus? Can't we see here the faith which he just said he missed in Israel? The evangelist is silent on the point, but this silence no doubt means this impetuous confidence in him was not the faith that leads to salvation. It is the miracle-worker that attracts them. But even to these Jesus does not refuse healing; he does not snap off the bruised reed (see 12:20). Even such childish and perhaps selfish eagerness can be the kernel of a mature and enlightened faith. We certainly have no right to pass judgment on it.

[17]. . . *so that the word spoken by the prophet Isaiah might be fulfilled: " he has taken away our infirmities and borne away our sicknesses."*

But Matthew sees even more : not just the miracles wrought on men, but the mystery of Jesus' person which shines forth in them. The prophet Isaiah had predicted of the Servant of God that he would take on himself all sicknesses and infirmities. He will be ready to bear our suffering instead of us. Jesus accepts the sicknesses of others, our infirmities, as his own. He draws them away from others and down on himself. And then they are " taken away." He not only has patience and resignation, but the power to transform and redeem. Just as he assumes the burden of our sins, he takes upon himself all suffering and turns it into blessing by his obedience. The mystery of his death and our re demption is beginning to be proclaimed.

Second Cycle of Miracles (8:18—9:13)

ON FOLLOWING CHRIST (8:18–22)

This passage and the following miracle on the lake (8:23-27) are closely connected with one another. First the hallmarks of true following are given, then the evangelist shows how they should prove themselves in practice in the event on the lake.

[18]*But when Jesus saw a great crowd of people around him, he gave the command to cross to the other shore.* [19]*And a scribe approached and said to him: " Master, I will follow you wherever you go."* [20]*And Jesus said to him: " The foxes have holes and the birds of the sky have nests; but the Son of Man has nowhere to lay his head."*

Capernaum lies on the Lake of Galilee. One day, Jesus notices the great crowd of people that is pressing around him and gives the order to sail across to the opposite side. This serves to prepare for the description of the crossing (8:23-27) and the little episode that follows is placed within this context. First comes a scribe who asks to be admitted into company of Jesus' followers. Respectfully, and at the same time correctly, he addresses Jesus as " Master," that is, teacher. He knows Jesus as a wandering rabbi with a circle of disciples to which one can offer oneself as a candidate. The disciple who appears later knows more about Jesus and chooses the majestic title of " Lord " to address him (8:21). The scribe shows great readiness; he is prepared to follow Jesus wherever he may go. This is nothing to be scoffed at.

Jesus' answer is neither a refusal nor an acceptance. All he does is to show what is in store for anyone who follows him. To become his disciple does not only mean to go to his school, as it were, to learn something. It means above all sharing his own life. His followers receive a share in the form of life lived by the Messiah, they are drawn into its being. That is primary, as Mark says about the calling of the apostles: " He called to himself those whom he would, and they came to him. Then he appointed twelve to be with him . . ." (Mk. 3:13f.).

Since Jesus left the house at Nazareth, he has renounced the security of home. That he lives in no house is an essential element of his new way of life. He does not start out on his various journeys from any fixed point, but lives the life of a wanderer. " He has nowhere to lay his head." This is not merely part of his call as preacher of the word. It is part of his self-emptying, of his life as the dedicated servant who denies himself the warmth and shelter of a home. We shall have to prepare ourselves for that before we decide. And we ought not be disappointed if he takes us at our word.

²¹*Another of the disciples said to him: " Lord, allow me first to go and bury my father." ²²But Jesus said to him: " Follow me, and let the dead bury their dead."*

The second, a disciple, asks to be allowed to do his duty as a devoted son on behalf of his aged father. To bury his father means that the speaker asks to stay at home until his father dies so that he can bury him and be quit of all his duties. That could last a long time. Jesus' answer sounds unusually sharp. The summons, " Follow me," means that he must act at once and join Jesus without delay. That is much more urgent and important than his duty as a son. " Let the dead bury their dead." Jesus brings life and is on the side of life. The words change their meaning in the sentence. The burying of the dead father means the real bodily burial. That this work should be done by the dead can be understood only metaphorically. Those who are spiritually dead, who have not listened to the call to life and remain obstinately in sin, are also gravediggers for others. All they can do is carry to the grave what is dying or already dead.

Does not the Lord disregard heartlessly here the duty which is inculcated by the fourth commandment? Does it not become quite incomprehensible, when in another place Jesus emphasizes this very duty, and rejects the hairsplitting of the scribes? (see 15 : 1–9). The grounds for so trenchant a demand must be very grave indeed. They are the urgency of the hour, the unique time fixed by God, which is here once and never comes back; the pressure of the coming kingship which spurs on Jesus himself without pause. Not a minute is to be lost. That holds good for the disciple as well as for the Master. But in this uncompromising fashion it holds good only for now, in the messianic age. Nevertheless, the church knows many alert and magnanimous souls who have been so struck by the call of God that everything else fades away and sinks into oblivion around them, so that they may be consumed by the flame that has taken root in their heart. Such there are in every age.

THE CALMING OF THE TEMPEST ON THE LAKE (8:23–27)

[23]*And when he entered the boat, his disciples accompanied him.* [24]*And behold, a violent storm blew up on the lake so that the boat was covered by the waves; but he was asleep.* [25]*And they came and woke him, saying: "Lord, save us, we are perishing."*

Jesus now embarks and his disciples " follow him." He goes first and the others follow after him. Thus the wording of the first lines continues the theme of the following of Christ, and inserts it into what took place on the lake.

In the middle of the lake a violent storm blows up, as it often does on the Sea of Galilee, which the surrounding mountains make a sort of cauldron. The small and not very seaworthy fishing boats are then in danger. The storms are enclosed in the cauldron, stir up the sea profoundly, and make proper steering almost impossible. The disciples, experienced fishermen, recognize the threatening danger immediately. Jesus is asleep in the middle of the storm. He is secure in God; the dire straits of existence do not affect him.

In trembling anxiety and filled with the terror of death, the disciples appeal to the master: " Lord, save us, we are perishing." It is a cry of despair, to be sure, but also of confidence. The only hope of escape they can see is the Lord in their midst. They have given themselves up for lost and find no help in their experience or their own strength. In this situation he alone could bring rescue. The cry, " We are perishing," has a spiritual sense over and above the literal one: we are lost, destroyed, we are finished, our whole life is over and done for, all hope is extinguished. We too experience the danger of death in such a way that as the peril threatens from without, all inner hope seems to vanish at the same time.

[26]*And he said to them: " Why are you afraid, you men of little faith?" Then he stood up, rebuked the winds and the sea, and there was a great calm.* [27]*But the people wondered and said: " Who is this, that even the winds and the lake obey him?"*

On being awoken, Jesus asks his friends in astonishment: " Why are you afraid, you men of little faith?" Faith is still feeble in anyone who is afraid. Faith drives out fear because it fills the whole man with God. The light of faith drives away the shadows of care and anxiety from every corner. They are " men of little faith," that is, faith is already there, otherwise they would not have expected help from him; but it is still scanty, otherwise they would not have sworn in their terror that they were lost. The disciple of Jesus often finds himself in such a situation. He believes, but not totally; he expects help from on high, but not complete rescue; he does not yet recognize that he is completely secure in the supporting hands of the Father, as Jesus has taught (see 6:25-34).

Jesus imposes restraint on the forces that were let loose, rebuking the wild storm and the raging seas. Suddenly all is still;

the disturbance seems to have fled like a specter. People now wonder "What sort of man is this?" Before this miracle, the astonishment was concerned with his authoritatively proclaimed message; now it is concerned with his mighty act, his power over storm and waves. The elements obey him just like demons and sickness. Must not man also obey him, since he possesses such authority? Is he not really Lord and Master, as the disciples address him? And is he not Lord of my life?

THE EXORCISM AT GADARA (8:28–34)

28And when he reached the other side in the land of the Gadarenes, two men who were possessed by demons came to him out of the tombs; they were very dangerous, so that no one could pass by that way. 29And behold, they cried out, "What have we to do with you, Son of God? Have you come here to torment us before the time?"

The opposite, that is to say, the eastern shore of the Sea of Galilee marks the boundary of the half heathen region of mixed population called the Decapolis, the ten cities. Gadara is one of these cities which were united in a league. When one climbs up from the lake, one crosses a mountainous region of many ravines through which narrow paths wind. The limestone has been eroded by water to form caves which provide refuge for tramps and nomads. Here, two men possessed by demons had found shelter. They lived apart from the city communities, having perhaps been driven away. Particularly wild and numerous demons had taken possession of them. The story is somewhat crude and bewildering. We must no doubt take into account that the narrative has been considerably influenced by popular story-telling. Matthew tells the story only in summary. He is concerned above all with the power of Jesus over the demons.

The two men rush to meet him and cry: " What have we to do with you, Son of God?" They recognize at once the radical hostility of the other, and indeed his special dignity. What remains hidden to men is clear to the sharp intelligence of the adversary. We have nothing to do with you, leave us in peace! " Have you come here to torment us before the time?" They seem to know that only a limited time has been granted to them. Their unhindered ravages in God's creation will come to an end. The day on which their power will be broken is not far away. Since the controversy in the desert (4:1-11), this certainly was clear to the kingdom of Satan.

30But there was a great herd of swine feeding not far from them. 31The demons besought him, saying, " If you drive us out, send us into the herd of swine." 32And he said to them, " Go!" Then they departed and entered into the swine; and behold, the whole herd rushed down the slope into the lake and died in the water.

The demons bargain for a delay with the skill of lawyers. If we are nearly done for, they argue, why do you torment us before the end comes upon us? At least let us go into these pigs so that we can run wild a little yet. In all seriousness this sounds rather grotesque, and it is still more strange that Jesus condescends to such bargaining. One might almost be inclined to take it as a flash of humour on the part of one who is exercising his authority and sovereign freedom which can allow itself certain exceptions.

³³*But the herdsmen fled; and when they had reached the city they proclaimed everything, including what had happened to the possessed.* ³⁴*And behold, the whole city came out to meet Jesus; and when they saw him, they besought him to depart from their territory.*

The people of the city were dismayed when they learned what Jesus had done, and they summoned him at least to leave their territory. The whole thing seems uncanny to them. Perhaps they fear further damage, beyond what they have already suffered by the loss of a whole herd of pigs. But this also means that Jesus can accomplish nothing there. Just as in his native town, he is also sent away from here. They want to have nothing to do with him. However, it is still not yet the " time of the nations." Jesus must first work in Israel, for he is sent " to the lost sheep of the house of Israel " (15:24). In spite of the uncanniness of the whole story, one thing is clear: the light has already shone upon the heathen for a brief space—like an announcement of the day that is near. But it is still dark.

THE HEALING OF THE PARALYTIC (9:1–8)

¹*And he went into the ship, crossed over, and came into his own city.* ²*And behold, some people brought to him a paralyzed man, lying on a stretcher. Jesus, seeing their faith, said to the paralyzed man: " Have courage, my son, your sins are forgiven."*

This event takes place back on the western side of the lake in his city, Capernaum (see 4:13). The crippled man is brought to Jesus, and this fact alone proclaims the faith of his helpers. A

new element now enters into the performance of miracles. Up
to this, all we have heard is that he healed men with all sorts
of diseases. But here he at once says: " Your sins are forgiven."
This is not to be taken as meaning that Jesus believed in an
immediate connection between the disease and a sin. In another
place, Jesus explicitly rejects the opinion of the scribes who held
that every sickness was the effect of a personal fault. However,
the man does suffer from two diseases: the disease in his failing
body, and the disease of sin which is destroying him from
within. The disease of sin is the graver of the two because no
human doctor can cope with it.

*And behold, some of the scribes said to each other: " He is
blaspheming." *And Jesus knew their thoughts and said: " Why
do you think evil in your hearts? *Which is easier to say, ' Your
sins are forgiven you,' or ' Stand up and walk'? *But that you
may know that the Son of Man has authority to forgive sins on
earth "—then he said to the paralyzed man: " Stand up, take
your bed, and go home to your house."*

The doctors of the law recognize correctly, as far as appearances
go, that a blasphemy against God has been uttered. Who can
arrogate to himself the divine power to forgive sins? Sin is after
all directed only against God. It is the careless neglect or the
deliberate transgression of what is precisely *his* command, and
in such a matter he alone is the competent judge. But here the
man who intervenes is not just anybody. Jesus proves it by a
clear piece of reasoning: You know yourselves, that it is harder
to forgive sins than to heal the body. Who could do the harder,
if he could not also do the easier? And vice versa, for if you
see with your own eyes that I can do away with external diseases,

is not that a proof that I am able to remove the inward illness? Though you do not start with any good will, will you not bow to the rational proof?

The " authority " of the Son of Man had been displayed in his teaching and felt with astonishment by the people (7:28). Here it shows itself in the power to take away sin. " On earth " means here and now, in this messianic age. It also indicates that what is forgiven on earth is also forgiven in heaven by God. What the Son of Man here does in virtue of the authority given him by God, he will later transfer to his apostles. Here the kingship of God arrives: life whole and sound takes control of a man—soul and body.

⁷And he stood up and went off to his house. ⁸When the crowds saw it, they were filled with fear, and gave praise to God who had given such authority to men.

That the cripple really stood up and went home seems to be a rather obvious inference from the story. Thus the story ends unexcitingly. The main thing which strikes the people is not the miraculous healing, but the fact that God " has given such authority to men." The action of God is emphasized here. How great must God be, since he does not guard his treasure jealously, but transfers full powers to men! Here it has been the Son of Man himself, but the point is not dwelt on; later it will really be mere men who will have power to forgive sins in the name of God. This miracle takes place every time our sins are forgiven. Do we remember that in this God is abandoning something that is his own in the strictest sense, and transfers to a man his own proper authority? Do we remember that it is always a grace freely bestowed?

JESUS AND THE TAX GATHERERS (9: 9–13)

This section puts before us first the call of the apostle Matthew (9:9), then a brief controversy with some Pharisees (9:10-12). The conclusion speaks of Jesus' being sent to sinners and so rounds off the whole section from 9:1 on.

⁹And as Jesus went on from there, he saw a man sitting at a customs' office, Matthew by name, and said to him: " Follow me!" And he stood up and followed him.

The call of the first four disciples was told in some detail earlier on. In the synoptic gospels, there is only one other apostle about whom the details of his becoming a disciple have been retained by tradition. This is " Levi, the son of Alphaeus," as Mark and Luke describe him (Mk. 2:14; Lk. 5:27). In the first gospel, this apostle is called Matthew, who, according to ancient tradition, wrote this gospel.

He is a collector of taxes, and therefore belonged to a despised class of men. In addition, a tax gatherer was unclean in the eyes of the Jews because he dirtied himself by trafficking in money; he was regarded as a notorious swindler and bloodsucker. Jesus called such a man. Once more this preference of God for what is insignificant and despised. The simple fishermen are joined by someone whose hand no one will shake. And like the others, he is a Galilean. This is a fine collection that Jesus now puts together. Are we too shocked by it?

¹⁰And now, as he was at table in the house, behold, many tax gatherers and sinners came and sat down with Jesus and his disciples.

The newly-called Matthew invites Jesus and his company to his house and puts a meal before them. This attracts other members of his craft and all sorts of publicity-shy people who know that they are held in the same contempt. They all come to the house and join in the meal. Those who have been kept at a distance by the haughty and have stayed in the shadows all their life at last dare to come forward, impelled by wonder and a timid hope. A great banquet is enjoyed by greasy tax gatherers and loose-living prostitutes. Jesus with his disciples is in the middle of them—unashamed of this doubtful company; to say nothing of the fact that he is not afraid of becoming unclean in the eyes of the law. What a picture!

[11]*And when the Pharisees saw it, they said to his disciples: "Why does your Master eat with the tax gatherers and sinners?"* [12]*But he heard them and said: "It is not the healthy that need a doctor, but the sick."*

The Pharisees approach the disciples to sound them out or to unsettle them: "Why does your master eat with the tax gatherers and sinners?" They find the procedure scandalous and repugnant. That can never be God's will or in accord with the law. And what finally will the teaching of such a master sound like, since he allows himself to give such scandal?

Jesus himself at once intervenes without waiting to be interrogated. His justification takes the form of a proverb, which is so wise and clear that it cannot be refuted: "It is not the healthy that need a doctor, but the sick." He does not say that the Pharisees are somehow to be counted among the healthy. Everything tells against that. All that he does is to emphasize that he has been sent to the ill. He is there to seek them out, to take charge of them, and to heal them like a doctor. And these very men who get no helping hand to draw them out of the mire are the sickest of all. Here is his place and his vocation.

[13]" *Go then and learn what this means: ' I will have mercy and not sacrifice.' For I did not come to call the just, but sinners."*

This saying gives a still wider basis to the justification of Jesus. Only Matthew gives the first part with the quotation from the prophet Osee. He means that what Jesus is doing is not an arbitrary trespass against the ordinances of God. It is not motivated merely by Jesus' own notions but has its roots in God himself. This is proved by the scriptures. God said through the prophets that he did not demand from men their sacrifices before all else, but human mercy. True worship of God must show itself in compassionate mercy, in care for the weak and fallen, in kindness and love.

That Jesus does not do this on his own initiative is affirmed again in the concluding phrase: " For I did not come." This " coming " always has a force of its own; it is the briefest expression of his calling. It indicates a movement from a starting point, from which he goes forth and whence he now comes, into this world of ours and into this moment of its time. It expresses more than " I am here." Behind his having come is this being sent by God, and with that mission is given the authority of God.

" (Not) to call the just but sinners." By the just we are not to understand those who mistakenly consider themselves as just. Jesus accepts the Jewish distinction between just and sinners. Their justice is not completely worthless and false but it is insufficient for many reasons, not least because the just separate themselves from the lowly " sinners " and leave them to their fate. The story of the Pharisee and the tax collector (Lk. 18 : 9–14) is a good illustration of this saying. As God thinks, so should men do: first of all, these models of piety, the Pharisees, who have to learn the alphabet of God's way of thinking like school-boys—mercy is what I want and not sacrifice. We are redeemed by mercy, and God desires to extend his redemption through our mercy.

Third Cycle of Miracles (9:14–34)

The last section of the greater complex begins with a controversy about the question of fasting. Jesus proclaims the present time as the messianic marriage feast and time of joy (9 : 14–17). To this corresponds the fact that the life of God penetrates into sick men: the daughter of Jairus and a woman are cured (9 : 18–26), two blind men are given their sight (9 : 27–31), and a mute spirit is expelled (9 : 32–34).

FASTING AND THE MESSIANIC ERA OF SALVATION (9:14–17)

[14]*The disciples of John then came to him and said: " Why do we and the Pharisees fast but your disciples do not fast?"*

This time the question is raised by the disciples of John, who, following his example, were leading an austere life of penance. They too, like the sect by the Dead Sea, tried to fulfill the will of God to the utmost. They are also like the Pharisees insofar as they imposed on themselves special efforts beyond what was generally commanded. If Jesus, as they do, teaches a higher perfection as is generally prescribed, why does he and his circle not also maintain a rigorous fast? They do not want to reproach Jesus with any laxity in the religious life. It is rather a matter of distrust as to whether he himself behaves in the way he teaches.

[15a]*And Jesus said to them: " Can the marriage-guests mourn as long as the bridegroom is with them?"*

Jesus' answer is once more perplexing. It does not appear to go into the heart of the question. The whole Sermon on the Mount shows that Jesus' thinking goes in quite a different direction. Here he gives a much more general answer. The inner meaning of fasting is mourning, but this is a time of joy. To keep to the metaphor: when the bridegroom invites his friends to the marriage, they do not come to a funeral service. Now the bridegroom is there and he gathers guests around him to celebrate his joy. Fasting has here no meaning at all; it would be in contradiction with this unique hour. Now is the time for jubilation and happiness.

[15b]*" But days will come when the bridegroom has been taken away from them, and then they shall fast."*

It will however not always be so, for the bridegroom is there only for a certain time until he is " taken away from them." The expression " taken away " is harsh and indicates a violent separation. Still under the veil of the metaphor, but unmistakably for the believing mind, Jesus here speaks for the first time of his painful end. In John, the Lord indeed says: " It is good for you that I go away; for if I do not go away, the Consoler will not come to you " (Jn. 16:7). And his presence is granted us in the Eucharist and in his Spirit: " For wherever two or three are gathered together in my name, there am I in the midst of them " (18:20). Nevertheless, it is painful that Jesus is not bodily among us, but has hidden himself until the time of the marriage of the Lamb (see Rev. 21:9ff.). In the period between removal and return fasting has taken on additional meaning. It is not only a work of penance, but an expression of mourning for being parted from the heavenly bridegroom and for being deprived of his bodily nearness.

[16]" *No one puts a piece of unshrunk cloth on an old garment; for the patch tears away still more of the garment, and an even greater tear results.* [17]*Nor do men pour new wine into old vessels; otherwise, the vessels burst and the wine is spilled and the vessels are destroyed. Rather, men pour new wine into new vessels, and both are preserved."*

Jesus adds two brief comparisons to his answer, each of them vivid and popular. They testify to practical good sense. No sensible housewife would dream of mending her wornout garment with a piece of raw new cloth. Otherwise what happens is that this patch does extra damage because it pulls at the older material around it. So it tears a hole much bigger than was there before and the dress becomes completely useless.

The second image says the same thing. The wine producer takes good care not to pour new fermenting wine into brittle containers. These will not withstand the pressure of the wine and will split open. The place for young wine is new vessels. Both pictures contrast the old and the new. Now is the time of the new thing, the time of the Messiah. It is fiery like young wine and fresh like untreated cloth. It has its own proper law, the law of joy and effervescent fullness. Old forms do not suit it; it will produce new ones. These two parables testify to bright hope and unshaken confidence in victory.

But doesn't this contradict other sayings which emphasize precisely the combination of the old with the new? Both things are to be maintained, but in different senses. The revelation brought by Jesus continues the Old Testament revelation in a straight line and fulfills it (5:17). The fulfillment, however, is in itself still something new, incomparable, and never to be repeated again. The time of the messianic work has its own proper fullness and explosive force such as never had existed before, and which will never be again until the end of the world. It is true to say of it: " Blessed are the eyes which see what you see " (Lk. 10:23). There are many examples in history of men who tried to apply these jubilant words of Jesus to their own actions. But that meant that they were abusing them. Our modest estimation of ourselves demands that we leave intact the uniqueness of the time of the Messiah.

THE WAKENING OF THE DEAD GIRL AND THE CURE OF THE WOMAN WITH THE FLOW OF BLOOD (9:18–26)

Following Mark, two miracle stories are here interwoven. The cure of the woman takes place without much notice in the middle of the throng which had gathered round the dead child of the overseer. For many details we must draw on the narrative of Mark (Mk. 5:21–43). Matthew restricts himself here to a few important elements.

[18]*While he was thus speaking to them, behold, an overseer approached, fell down before him and said: " My daughter has just died; but come and lay your hand upon her and she will come back to life." *[19]*And Jesus arose and followed him with his disciples.*

We have already heard of a heathen officer and now we hear of a Jewish president of a synagogue. He held the highest

religious office in the locality and was responsible for supervis-
ing divine service and for the upkeep of the house of worship.
His daughter has just died. His grief leads him to Jesus and full
of confidence he asks him to bring her back to life. If he lays his
wonder-working hand on her, that will be enough. The Lord is
ready at once and sets out with his disciples. In view of this faith,
it seems that all is not lost in Israel.

*²⁰And behold, a woman who had been suffering from a flow of
blood for twelve years came forward and touched from behind
the hem of his garment. ²¹For she said to herself: " If I only
touch his garment, I shall be healed." ²²But Jesus turned around,
looked at her, and said: " Have courage, daughter, your faith
has healed you." And the woman was healed from that hour.*

In the middle of the throng an unhappy woman succeeds in
touching Jesus' garment from behind. Her faith is great, even
though it announces itself in an almost magical action. But even
this faith is welcomed by Jesus, this wordless, simple confidence,
which can only present itself in a gesture. In contrast to Mark,
Matthew shows clearly, however, that it is Jesus' words which
cause the cure, his will and his imperious utterance, not a magical transmission of healing force into the sick body. Thereby, he
gives a more spiritual significance to Mark's text which has the
naïveté of popular storytelling. He averts the misunderstanding
by which Jesus could be seen merely as a wonder worker with
superhuman powers. It is important to note such matters within
the framework of the gospels themselves. There is a regulating
force at work among the sacred writers, and the full truth comes
to light only when all the narratives are looked at together.
    Jesus says with emphasis that it is her faith which has healed

her. Faith always remains the presupposition and the foundation of God's saving action on man. Faith can no doubt take various forms—primitive and undeveloped, or purified and spiritual. But it is always on the march and always growing, from faith to faith (Rom. 1:17), that is, from the elementary forms already present into a faith which is ever more deeply known and more thoroughly lived.

[23]And when Jesus entered the house of the overseer and saw the flute players and the noisy crowd, [24]he said: " Go away! For the girl is not dead but sleeping." And they laughed him to scorn. [25]But when the crowd had been put out, he went in and took her hand and the girl stood up. [26]And the news of this went abroad into all that region.

Jesus has reached the house and remarks with obvious displeasure the noise of the mourning women, the flute players, and a crowd of people who were lamenting the dead with loud cries after oriental custom. This unbridled noise entirely contradicts the simple way of Jesus and of his aid. He orders the crowd to leave the house. They laughed at him on account of the reason which he had given: that the whole noisy parade was entirely out of place since the girl was only sleeping. Does Jesus say this to have a plausible reason for stopping the noise? That would hardly be in character. He seems to mean that for him and for God's power this death has no more importance than a light sleep. So also at the raising of Lazarus he says: " Lazarus, our friend, is asleep. But I go to wake him up " (Jn. 11:11). Death is no insuperable obstacle to God; the wall that divides it from life is a thin one. The people do not understand this, and so they deride him with foolish laughter. Things look quite different in the eyes of God than in the experience of men. Only when we train ourselves to see things with the eyes of God do we get the proper picture. And then even death loses its terror. The sequel is briefly narrated. Jesus simply takes the girl by the hand and she is at once able to get up and is as healthy as before. This is the first time that the evangelist narrates a raising from the dead. The easy way in which it takes place is astonishing. It seems to be in no way unusual or unheard-of, but something quite normal for him who brings life.

The Healing of Two Blind Men (9:27-31)

[27]And as Jesus went on from there, two blind men followed him who cried out, saying: " Have mercy on us, Son of David!" [28]But when he came into the house, the blind men came to him, and Jesus said to them: " Do you believe that I can do this?" They said to him, " Yes, Lord." [29]Then he touched their eyes and said: " According to your faith, so be it done to you." [30]And their eyes were opened. And Jesus threatened them, saying, " See to it that no one knows." [31]But when they went out, they spoke of him throughout the whole region.

Jesus had healed two possessed at Gadara, now it is two blind men. When they tell about the miracle, their statements will support one another. For according to the rule given in the Old Testament, a statement is held to be true and proved only when it is affirmed by two witnesses. Their faith speaks. " Have mercy on us," they say. They do not ask in so many words for the power of sight. What they entreat him to do is to show mercy. If Jesus turns to them in mercy, then they will also be freed from their suffering. The first and decisive thing according to their faith is this gracious attention to them.

Jesus examines them to see if their faith is also rightly adjusted and he asks them if they are convinced he has the power to do the miracle. They agree without reserve and thereupon they are healed. At the end, the Lord gives them strict orders not to tell anyone about it. What was done to them should remain between them and God. But neither of them pays the least attention to the order, and everywhere they go they tell of him who cured them.

This contrast is strange. Neither of them obeys Jesus; they do the opposite. We meet such " commands of secrecy " in many other places in the synoptics, especially in Mark. Some of them are imposed on the healed, others on the disciples. In Mark they serve to conceal the true messianic dignity of Jesus from the great masses. Matthew doesn't have this intention; hence at this very place the blind men address Jesus as " Son of David " without being forbidden to do so. Matthew no doubt means to tell us first and foremost that Jesus did not display himself as a sensational miracle man but did everything he could to avert misunderstanding of his mission. The glory should belong to God alone.

The Healing of a Mute (9:32-34)

[32]*But when they were gone away, behold, some people brought to him a mute who was possessed.* [33]*And when the demon had been driven out, the mute began to speak. And the crowds were amazed and said: " Nothing like this has ever been seen in Israel!"* [34]*But the Pharisees said: " By the ruler of demons he drives out demons."*

A second healing follows at once. A possessed man is brought to him, one who is also dumb. After the miracle two opinions are expressed. The crowds affirm that nothing like that had ever been known in Israel, that is, not only in the land of Palestine but in the history of the people. In the past many wonderful things had happened. God had often revealed himself by signs and demonstrations of his power. Prophets too, like Elias and Eliseus, had performed miracles. Now the people also testify that here " there is more than the temple " (see 12 : 6) and " more than the prophets " (see 16 : 14-16).

The Pharisees think differently. Their pretensions go so far that they make the monstrous reproach that it is with the help of devilish powers that Jesus works his miracles. They accuse him of being allied to the chief of the kingdom of demons and of deriving his strength from him. Here we can see the abyss which is already opening its jaws between Jesus and his opponents. It is no longer a matter of a controversy about a text of scripture or a religious custom, but of an irreconcilable opposition. God and Satan had been opposed in the duel in the wilderness (4 : 1-11). The Pharisees show by their charge that they are on the side of the evil one.

Thus the description of the miracles of Jesus ends on a shrill note of discord. The double verdict at the end can also be applied to the whole cycle of wonders from 8 : 1 on. Nothing like it had ever been seen in Israel—that is a general testimony to the unique and glorious revelation which has been made in the work of the Messiah. He drives out demons by the power of the ruler of the demons—that is the opposing testimony of his enemies, springing from ill will and deliberate misinterpretation. Thus even the miracles of Jesus can be misunderstood. They too need to meet with good will and the readiness to believe. They are signs which are to be recognized; but they are also signs which can be contra-dicted. God does not force us, not even by miracles. The decision is made at the moment when we answer the question which faith puts to us: " Who is this man?"

The Teaching on Discipleship (9:35—11:1)

The second great discourse in the gospel of Matthew deals with dis-cipleship. It is directed to the twelve apostles who are regarded as prototypes of every true disciple of Jesus. The discourse is composed of four sections: the call of the apostles and their mission (10:1-16); their destiny of persecution (10:17-25); the warning to profess the faith (10:26-33); the decision on behalf of Jesus and parting from family (10:34-39). The discourse is introduced by a prologue and ended by an epilogue (10:40—11:1).

The Introduction (9:35-38)

[35]*And Jesus went about all the towns and villages, teaching in their synagogues and proclaiming the gospel of the kingship; and he healed every disease and every infirmity.*

First we read a summary account of the activity of Jesus in the formula in which the evangelist has already given it in 4:23. The words are almost the same. Matthew gives two indications of place: Jesus goes around to the towns and villages and teaches in the synagogues. The meaning is that there should be no-where that people did not learn of his message. And further: Jesus makes use of the official method of teaching, that is, the address to the congregation at divine service in the synagogues. The evangelist knows, of course, that Jesus also taught in the

open air and in many situations which suddenly presented themselves. But he wants to insist that the Messiah is sent " to the lost
sheep of the house of Israel " (10:6), and that he goes about his
instruction in the legal, orderly way.

Matthew also gives two indications of what was being done:
Jesus teaches and heals. He proclaims the gospel of the kingship and heals every illness that he meets. This dual aspect of
Jesus' work is sketched once more (see 4:23). We are also reminded of the structure which put the Sermon on the Mount
(ch. 5–7) into conjunction with the cycle of miracles (8:1—9:34).

³⁶*But when he saw the crowds, he was filled with compassion
for them, for they were harried and scattered, like sheep that
have no shepherd.*

Jesus sees the people tired and worn out, leaderless and neglected.
For they have no shepherd to lead them to rich pastures and
guard them well and faithfully. Ezekiel, speaking in God's
name, had already accused the official shepherds of Israel, the
princes and governors, of feeding themselves instead of the flock
(Ez. 34:2). God himself was to exercise in the future the office
of shepherd (Ez. 34:11ff.). Now, in Jesus, whom Peter later
calls the " Chief Shepherd " (1 Peter 5:4), God has come nigh
for the " lost sheep of the house of Israel." Peter looks farther
afield to include the shepherds of the new people of God, the
apostles and their mission.

³⁷*Then he said to his disciples: " The harvest is great, but the
workers are few. ³⁸Pray therefore the Lord of the harvest that
he send workers into his harvest."*

Jesus speaks of the harvest. That is an ancient picture for the completion of all things. The prophets invented it; Jesus takes it up. He sees the waving fields ripe for mowing. For he has been announced as one " whose shovel is in his hand, and who will cleanse his threshing floor to bring his wheat into his barns but to burn the chaff in unquenchable fire " (3:12). With the coming of the kingship of God the sorting out begins—the judgment, which is already taking place in the decision of the individual. But there are few workers. The reapers are scarce; there is a shortage of such men who will call for decision. Jesus sees an immense task before him, a task which demands the cooperation of men.

Therefore there follows the exhortation to pray to the Lord of the harvest, the great God, that he may call harvest workers for the ripe fields. Why does Jesus exhort his disciples to ask God for this? Does he not himself call the apostles into his service in order that they may help with the great messianic work? Jesus confesses that it is ultimately God who calls them to the service of his message and sends them just as he himself has been sent by the Father (10:40). But he indicates something else as well: this prayer must always be offered as long as the eschatological harvest time, the time of the End, goes on. The communities in the apostolic church did so—especially, no doubt, the community in which Matthew himself lived—and this prayer must always be made in our own days too.

The Call of the Apostles and Their Mission (10:1–16)

THE TWELVE APOSTLES (10:1–4)

¹*And he called his twelve disciples to himself and gave them*

authority over the unclean spirits, to drive them out; and to heal every sickness and every infirmity. ²But the names of the twelve apostles are: First Simon, who is called Peter, and Andrew his brother, and James, the son of Zebedee, and John, his brother, ³Philip and Bartholomew, Thomas and Matthew, the tax gatherer, James, the son of Alphaeus, and Thaddaeus, ⁴Simon, the Cananean, and Judas, the Iscariot, who also delivered him up.

The twelve apostles occur here as a college which has already been chosen and belongs permanently to Jesus. The choice itself is not narrated at all by Matthew. Jesus gives them authority over the demons and over all sicknesses. Later there comes as well the charge to preach (10:7). The evangelist uses the same expressions as he uses to describe Jesus' own authority, and thus shows that the apostles are to be exactly like him—they are to be the prolongation of his mission. They will work as he did, and confirm their word by miracles.

Then follow the names of the twelve apostles. Significantly, Simon, with the surname of Peter, stands in the first place. Only much later do we hear how Simon came to have this name (16:18). Here we have an official catalogue, a list of officeholders in which this surname must be given. First the two pairs of brothers are mentioned whose call has already been described at the beginning. The church certainly looked on them from the earliest days as the first to be called (4:18–22). Only two of the next mentioned are described more precisely in the gospel: the tax collector Matthew (Levi), who was called from his place at the customs to take up the following of Christ (9:9), and Judas, the betrayer. In the gospel of John we read more about Philip and Bartholomew and Thomas. This is not very much. One can understand how legend tried later to fill in the gaps which the gospels leave open. But the gospels were not written to satisfy curiosity and pious feelings. In their brevity, they are always directed to one figure—Jesus, the Messiah. Everyone, even if he holds the highest office, even an apostle, exists only with reference to Jesus and holds everything he has from him.

The names allow us to form many conclusions about the composition of the circle of the apostles. Greek names stand beside Jewish ones; different regions of Palestine may be envisaged for their origin; simple fishermen appear beside a member of the radical zealot party (Simon the Cananean) and disciples of John the Baptist (James and John). It seems to be a very mixed crowd that Jesus gathers about him, not a set of docile and easily-managed followers, but at the same time, hardly flatterers who will do anything to please. Jesus had a hard time with them, and to all appearances, very little success. But when they were really converted and when the Holy Spirit had inflamed them, they became death-defying witnesses and the pillars of the foundation on which the church arose.

That Judas too was one of them is one of the most horrifying mysteries of all time. The borders between the kingdom of God and the realm of Satan lie close together. The betrayer from the circle of intimates becomes the instrument of the evil one. Jesus has given himself over to these men whom he honored with so high a mission; and he took on himself the risk of being given over to death by one of them.

The Mission of the Apostles (10:5–16)

⁵Jesus sent out these twelve and gave them the command: " Do not take the path to the heathen and do not enter any cities of the Samaritans. ⁶Go rather to the lost sheep of the house of Israel."

Now comes the mission. The Lord gives precise directions: first, as regards where they are to go, then, as regards what they are to say. They are to go neither to the Samaritans who were looked upon as half pagan and whose attitude was hostile, nor to the heathens, but only to the Israelites. It is not thereby decreed that heathens and Samaritans are to have no part in the kingship of God and the blessings of the messianic times. Jesus merely lays down the order which salvation is to take according to God's fixed plan, which is—from the Jews to the gentiles. This is the way that Jesus himself understood his mission and, as can be seen from the gospels, he kept to it strictly: " I am not sent except to the lost sheep of the house of Israel " (15 : 24). He may have found this restriction difficult. But this obedience forms part of the self-emptying of the Son of God by which we are redeemed. This is something which must be kept in mind in all apostolic and pastoral effort. What matters is not the number of works undertaken or the size of the sphere of influence, but that we do what is God's will in the narrow circle fixed by him.

In their later missions this rule no longer holds good for the apostles and the door to the heathens is thrown wide open. Here however these words have to be put down so that every Jew can see clearly that God has first offered salvation to Israel. The Messiah and his envoys have done nothing but obey him. If, then, the Gentiles have found the faith which Israel has refused (see 8 : 10–12), the Jews remain without excuse.

[7]" *Go and proclaim:* ' *The kingdom of heaven is at hand.*' [8a]*Heal the sick, wake the dead, cleanse the lepers, drive out demons."*

The apostles are to make the same proclamation that Jesus had made: " The kingdom of heaven is at hand." It is the time of the great harvest, of God's unique approach to his people, time of fulfillment and therefore time of conversion and repentance. The authority which the apostles have received is also to be exercised in the healing of sicknesses, even in the raising of the dead and the expulsion of evil spirits—and so they will be like Jesus. Jesus sums up what we have already fully heard: the healing of all sicknesses (4:23f; 8:17), the raising of the dead (9:18f, 23–26), the cleansing of leprosy (8:1–4) and the expulsion of demons (4:24; 8:16, 28–34; 9:32). We hear very seldom that the apostles did such things in the time of Jesus. Later however this authority is powerfully developed; the Acts of the Apostles in particular narrate such miracles which Peter worked in the name of Jesus (Acts 3:1–10; 5:12–16; 9:31–43). In apostolic times, the time of the primitive church, the preaching is accompanied by signs and wonders. This comes from the special powers with which the apostles were endowed by the Lord for their mission. It happens from time to time later on, especially in the lives of the saints. There the power to work miracles is a new and particular gift of God, but no longer connected with a definite office and a definite era as in the apostolic church.

8b" *Freely have you received, freely shall you give.* 9*Do not aim at gaining gold or silver, or at having copper in your purses.* 10*Have no sack of provisions for the way, nor two cloaks, nor shoes nor a staff; for the laborer is worthy of his support.*"

The proclamation of the gospel is to be kept free from all suspicion of avarice. Jesus imparts his gifts without being paid, and so also are they to be passed on. This principle remained in apostolic times that the missionary worked without payment; his well-being was the concern of the faithful. The preaching can

inflame hearts only when, as in the case of Jesus, it is not performed for the sake of gain. The apostles are to earn no income,
neither in coins of gold or silver, nor even the less valuable copper
coins. When they go on their travels, they must rely entirely on
God. He will support them as he looks after the birds and the
lilies of the field. If only they give themselves entirely to his service, God will take care of all the rest.

Simplicity and frugality are also the distinguishing marks of the
equipment which Jesus prescribes. They are to leave at home the
knapsacks that would be useful for food and other provisions for
the journey; and they are not to take a change of cloak with them.
Strangely enough, this applies also to shoes and the walker's stick
which are not precisely luxuries. We are to understand by shoes,
perhaps, strong, well-made footwear which will last a long time
and do for mountains, not the light sandals which are indispen-
sable in the pitted limestone hills. But why no walking stick? Is
it to be left behind to ease their load? At any rate, the utmost
frugality is demanded. " For the laborer is worthy of his support ". Anything that is required beyond the absolute minimum will be given to the missionaries while on the way. Indeed,
they have a claim on it, which is later demanded. Paul is the
exception. The apostolic rule survives even to our own days,
though in a different form. The communities support all those
who minister to them with the word of God and the sacraments.
Each of the parties must keep in mind that it is a relationship of
giving and taking in a brotherly spirit; and also, that it is
restricted by the apostolic rule to what is necessary.

[11]*"When you enter a city or a town find out which of the inhabitants is worthy in it and stay there until you go on further. [12]But
when you enter a house, then pronounce the greeting. [13]And if*

the house is worthy of it, your peace will come upon it; but if it is not worthy of it, then your peace will return to you. [14]*And if they do not receive you, and do not listen to your words, then go out of the house or that city and shake the dust from your feet.* [15]*Truly, I tell you: It will be more bearable for the land of Sodom and Gomorrha on the day of judgment than for that city."*

The next section contains Jesus' directions for the missionaries' quarters. When they enter a town they must first inquire which house would be suitable for them. Once they have found it, they are to stay there as long as they are working in that place. This implies a prohibition against their taking up quarters in several houses, going from one to another. In early missionary times it seems that unhappy experiences resulted from such changes, for which reason the rule given by Jesus was also applied later. Otherwise there could be cases of jealousy and envy; all sorts of gossip and rumors could start to the disadvantage of the message.

When they enter a house they are to pronounce their greeting. This is the greeting " Peace," such as has remained the custom in the East down to our own days. Luke gives it more clearly : " When you enter a house, say first, ' Peace be to this house ' " (Lk. 10:5). When they come as envoys of the kingship, the wishing of peace is no longer merely a polite formula. What the messengers bring with them, the power to heal and the might to work wonders by virtue of the kingship of God, will make its entry into that house. It is the peace of God which descends upon the house so favored. But if the house is not ready for God and his messengers, if it does not respond with joy and eagerness to the greeting of peace, then the envoys will be powerless. The peace that they have wished and offered will return to them. When the priest comes to the sick, he says " Peace to this house."

Hitherto, Jesus was speaking of a single house, or rather, of the household, the family with children, grandparents, and all who help. A house can refuse the offer of peace. But that can also happen to a whole city; it can reject the messengers, not letting them in at all or not listening to them. Failure can ensue, as Jesus himself experienced, and most painfully of all in his hometown of Nazareth (13:53-58). It was the lot of Paul, above all, on many occasions. When that happens the messengers are not to give way to melancholy complaints and not even to blame themselves; they are not to search for grounds for excuse or pin their hopes on new efforts. The offer of God comes only once and for all. If the hour is not recognized, it never comes again. They are simply to go away, and even to shake the dust of that place from their feet as a sign that God and they themselves will have nothing more to do with them. Everything depends on the moment of decision which is granted once and cannot be repeated.

However, punishment will not be wanting. Sodom and Gomorrha were razed to the ground by God's anger. But the sinful inhabitants of these cities will be let off more lightly at the judgment than the people of any of the cities which now disregard the call of God. We must keep such words in mind ourselves if we are to understand properly the trial of Jesus later on.

16*"Behold, I send you like sheep among wolves; be you therefore as wise as serpents and as innocent as doves."*

Wolf and sheep have already occurred as images: the false prophets break into the sheepfold with the pious-looking sheepskin on them (7:15). Here the metaphor is reversed: Jesus sends the disciples like guileless sheep into a pack of wolves. They seem to be exposed to savagery. The kingship of God is attested in weakness, in Jesus as in his messengers. It is at its mightiest where it reveals itself in the weakest, as St. Paul says: "For the power (of God) comes to perfection in weakness" (2 Cor. 12:9). The disciples are to face this soberly, and neither avoid the danger nor make for it boldly. Jesus combines two comparisons from animal life. The serpent is proverbially sly and deceitful (see Gen. 3:1). We are not to stumble clumsily into every danger; we are not to be the victims of every trick and snare. Prudence is called for—that combination of human adaptability to life and the sense of what is right and necessary.

But the disciples are also to be "innocent as doves." That undoubtedly does not mean that they are to be foolishly naïve and unsuspicious. They must be sincere. Prudence is not to become refined slyness or tricky strategy. That can only be avoided if the messengers are quite sincere and do not try to conceal their real purpose and their true interests. People must feel that what matters to them is God and never human advantage. Such prudence and innocence together will help them to stand fast even against opposition and give testimony to God.

A Destiny of Persecution (10:17-25)

[17]" But be on your guard against men; for they will deliver you over to the courts and scourge you in their synagogues. [18]And you will be brought before governors and kings for my sake as testimony for them and for the heathens."

This section begins on a note that has already been heard: " Be on your guard against false prophets " (7:15). Here the disciples are warned against men in general. Human ways and calculations will meet them as enemies, especially among the Jews, among whom they must carry out their first mission. They will be brought before the local courts, the minor sanhedrins, and suffer the punishment of scourging. Indeed, even the authorities of the country, Roman governors and the Jews' own kings of the family of Herod, will be called in to deal with them. Before them, they will have to give an account of themselves. But that will become a testimony for Jews and for heathens. They stand accused for the sake of Jesus; they give testimony to him in the very process of being charged and condemned with a loyalty which endures to the end in the face of men's contempt. It is this that will be an amazing testimony, a revelation of the glory of God in the weakness of man.

[19]*" But when they deliver you up, do not be anxious about what or how you are to speak; for what you are to say will be granted to you in that hour.* [20]*For it is not you who speak, but the Spirit of your Father who speaks through you."*

In the courts, they must not rely on their own prudence and be anxious about finding the right words. If they stand there as witnesses, their whole mind will set upon one thing only, namely, that divine testimony comes out pure and clear. And then the Holy Spirit of God will inspire them with the words they have to utter. He is in fact the helper, the Advocate of Christians who takes them under his protection and defends them against their accusers. He who dwells in the heart will speak from the heart; as we read about St. Stephen: " But they could not resist the wisdom and the Spirit with which he spoke " (Acts 6:10).

[21]*" But brother will deliver up brother to death and the father his child; and children will rise up against their parents and put*

them to death. ²²And you will be hated by all men for my name's sake; but he who perseveres to the end will be saved."

Persecutors are found even within one's own family where hatred divides the closest relatives (10:34–36). The prophet Micah had announced it among the terrors of the last days: perversion of mind and confusion of heart will be so great that the natural bonds of the family will burst asunder. And thus Israel will be ripe for judgment (Mic. 7:6). So too in Jesus' description: hatred will break out everywhere his envoys come. The prediction " You will be hated by all men," sounds absolutely terrifying.

In this situation there is only one thing to do: to be steadfast until the end, to hold out undismayed through all assaults, disappointments and failure. That is no small thing. But Jesus promises such a disciple that he will be saved. His eternal salvation is assured and he need have no fears about it. In how much silent heroism and unnoticed loyalty will this word of Jesus have been proved true.

²³*" But when they persecute you in one city, then flee to the next. For truly, I tell you, you will not be finished with the cities of Israel, till the Son of Man comes."*

It has already been said that the disciples are to go on at once when they are not welcomed and listened to (10:14). The same holds good for persecution. The hunt will be up for them. Then they must prudently make use of the possibilities of flight—from one city to another—and not be misled by false heroism into seeking danger and exposing themselves to it. Here too they are to be wise as serpents (10:16).

There is no reason to despair, not even in this seemingly hopeless situation. Just as the Holy Spirit will come to their aid when they are haled before the courts, so Jesus here promises them consolation by his own coming. You are not bereft of hope when you are exposed to the blows of your enemies: for I am at hand! My coming to deliver you, to free you from your tribulations—that will be the last word.

Jesus speaks of the *Son of Man* as though he were someone else. He hides himself behind this designation which properly speaking signifies only " man," a " human being," that is, something quite ordinary. This title actually conceals more than it reveals. The greatest thing that is said about the Son of Man is that he will come on the clouds of heaven to execute divine judgment. In our text his " coming " is to be understood in this sense. In our darkness and tribulation where we are stripped of all earthly consolation and all human hopes, we know that he will surely come and save his own.

²⁴" *The disciple is not above his master, nor the servant above his lord.* ²⁵ᵃ*It is enough for the disciple that he should be like his master, and the servant like his lord.*"

Jesus takes as a comparison the relationship between pupil and master, servant and lord. The relationship in each case is that of superiority and subordination. As long as the learner remains a pupil he is under the master. Both of them, disciple and servant, are in a position of dependence, receiving their doctrine or their orders from someone greater, who knows more than they or who has more power. These images are not chosen at random, but depict the existing relationship of the disciples to Jesus. They have to accept his doctrine and carry out his commands. This relationship will always remain in force since Jesus always remains their teacher and Lord. With regard to him, they have never finished their studies.

Hence the lesser must be content to undergo the same experiences as his master. " He should be like his master." He can hope for nothing more or better. What many parents say: " Our children will be better off than us," will not be true of them. On the contrary, the greatest possible resemblance to his life is also the closest possible intimacy with him. The disciple will be so much better pupil, the more he is like the teacher, so much better a servant, the more he is like his Lord.

25b" *If they have called the master of the house Beelzebub, how much more the members of his household!"*

The " master of the house " is Jesus himself. He describes himself only here by this rare word. To understand it properly one must no doubt read it along with the promise to Peter: " On this rock I will build my church " (16:18). The house built by Jesus himself is the community of the faithful which he gathers. In this house, he is the Lord, the *Kyrios* who reigns with fullness of authority. It is against him that blasphemies were uttered; it is he who was accused of a pact with the devil (9:34; 12:24). We, too, have to count on such things, and we ought not be astonished at contemptuous words and slanderous attacks.

Exhortation to Profess the Faith (10:26-33)

26" *Be not therefore afraid of them; for nothing is concealed that will not be revealed, and nothing is hidden that will not be known.* 27*What I say to you in darkness, repeat in the light; and* *what you hear whispered in your ears, proclaim from the house-tops."*

Jesus often warns, " Be on your guard," " Beware " (7 : 15; 10 : 17). But then again he says, as here, " Be not afraid." Both things are necessary, first prudence in knowing the enemy and in sober assessment of the threat he implies; and then fearless steadfastness under attack. Faith drives out fear. To know that we belong to the Messiah and suffer his own destiny makes us bold and courageous.

The beginnings of the new thing that Jesus has brought are modest enough. Anyone would think that he could easily crush the tender seed of corn under his feet. But what now lives silently and in concealment will manifest itself triumphantly. Jesus comes in the guise of the lowly servant of God to do his work—and then he will be revealed as the hope of the gentiles (see 12 : 17–21). Now he speaks in obscurity, but they are to speak out in the light. What is whispered in their ears, far away from the people and unknown to the public, is to be preached by them in the full light of day to all hearers. Whether they are received or rejected by men, the same law holds good. The good news will always be attested by them, and their light will finally shine out in triumph like the morning sun.

[28]*" And do not be afraid of those who kill the body, but cannot kill the soul; fear him rather, who can destroy soul and body in hell.* [29]*Are not two sparrows sold for a penny? And not one of them falls to the ground without your Father's leave.* [30]*But as for you, the very hairs of your head are numbered.* [31]*Be not then afraid! You are worth more than many sparrows."*

" Be not afraid!" That is repeated like a refrain in this passage

(10:26, 28, 31). The power of man is limited and though it may rage against you, it can only attack your earthly life (= the body). No human might can destroy what makes up your true worth, your hope of heavenly life (= the soul). The loss of earthly life has no connection with the loss of eternal life which is destruction in hell. But there is one who possesses power over both. He can do both as he pronounces judgment: deliver the whole man to hell, or call him to blessedness. He it is that we should fear.

Is this picture of God not terrifying? But here only one side of the picture of God is lit up; the other will be mentioned at once in the next verses: God's fatherly care, his tender closeness to man. But the word that speaks of his lordly majesty is also there and it must be allowed to stand. Only when we see God as so great and recognize his omnipotence, even over our very life, does his fatherliness gain its full force.

Sparrows are cheap because they can be found in great quantities; this is also true of the wild lilies of the field (see 6:28–30). Even in the most minute event the hand of God is at work, though all that happens is that a sparrow falls from its nest or is shot down by a boy. How much more will God be with you, and be concerned with anything that may happen to you? The very hairs on your head have been counted! So precise is his knowledge, so careful his love as he turns his eyes on you! Just as the lover knows every detail about the beloved, and notices every change at once, so God with us. There is really no reason to be afraid of men who cannot do the least thing without the Father's knowing about it.

[32]" *Everyone then, who confesses me before men, I will confess also before my Father in heaven.* [33]*But everyone who denies me before men, I will deny also before my Father in heaven.*"

He who is brought before a court of justice—for the sake of faith in Jesus—must also confess there. His acknowledgement of Jesus is not to be confined to times when he is not met with contradiction or threats. Faith will prove itself precisely in the moment of decision and when everything goes wrong. He who proves himself in this way before human judgment may be full of confidence before divine judgment. For there Jesus Christ himself will appear as the counsel for the defense to plead for him before the Father. Jesus says with emphasis: " before my Father." The roles will be reversed. Jesus was, so to speak, accused before the human court, but defended by his witnesses. Now it is the other way round: the witness is accused before the divine judgment, and Jesus defends him. A mysterious exchange is made from one side to the other. What an eloquent picture for Jesus' office of mediator!

The same thing is also true the other way round. Christ will not grant his aid before the Father in heaven to anyone who disassociates himself from Christ before men. Christ in turn will disavow him and deny him, perhaps with as hard a word as we read in the Sermon on the Mount: " But then I will say to them: 'I have never known you; depart from me, you evil-doers'" (7:23).

But has not the Father given judgment over to the Son? Is his role of defense counsel the same as he has as Judge at the end of time (see 3:11f.; 7:22f.)? The imagery varies in scripture. What in one place is attributed to the Father, in another is done by the Son; and what is described as the work of the Son is often ascribed to the Holy Spirit. The mysteries of God can never be comprehensively expressed in one sentence or in one image. Jesus is at once the *Kyrios* to whom the Father has given all things (see 28:18), and the obedient servant who only does the will of the Father (see 12:18). The saying given here is completed by the

other in Mark : " But whoever is ashamed of me and my words
before this adulterous and sinful generation, of him will the Son
of Man also be ashamed when he comes in the glory of his Father
with the holy angels " (Mk. 8 : 38). Both sayings affirm that one's
eternal destiny is decided by one's attitude to him—and to him
alone.

Decision for Jesus and Separation from one's own

[34]" *Do not believe that I am come to bring peace to the earth; I
am not come to bring peace, but the sword.*"

In impassioned lament, the prophet Micah had described the
corruption of his people : the rule of law had been abolished, the
administrators of justice had become takers of bribes, indeed, a
general disintegration had disrupted even family bonds. Every
man the enemy of all—that could have been the title of his
lament (Mic. 7 : 1-7). The prophet sees the judgment of God
already at work in this very corruption. His contemporaries
already experience in their own persons the consequences of their
apostasy from the Lord.

Jesus has the words of the prophet in mind. The judgment of
God, which Micah already saw working out, has entered upon
the hour of decision. His coming has brought that about. He has
been sent to bring the news of the kingship of God. Moreover,
with his own person it already arrives. It comes in the form of
division, as a *sword*. That is the sword of judgment which
separates good and evil, those who believe and those who refuse
the sword of decision before which man is placed. This is the
first thing that Jesus says here.

The opposite to this is peace. This can only mean a peace which is in contrast to this hour of decision. And such a peace would be a standstill peace which left everything in its old place, with the fronts not clearcut and the opposition between God and Satan plastered and papered over. It would be ultimately peace between God and Satan, which can never be and must never be.

35" *For I am come to set a man against his father, the daughter against her mother, and the daughter-in-law against her mother-in-law;* 36*and a man's enemies will be those of his own household."*

His word is sharper than a sword, as the Epistle to the Hebrews says about the word of God in general (Heb. 4:12). It penetrates bone and marrow and divides in the inner man our false desires from true fear of God. It can also strike at the family and set parents and children, daughter-in-law and mother-in-law, against one another. The boundary always runs along the place where the decision is called for: for or against God. The consequence of this can be separation from others, even from those most dear. This is not to be taken to mean that the disciple of Jesus may take up a hostile or implacable attitude. But he must reckon with the fact that his decision may bring down upon him the enmity even of his own relatives. This is no doubt the most painful experience in the following of Christ. But these words may never be misused to distort the message of peace which the church brings, or to justify one's own shortcomings with regard to an unbelieving family.

37" *He who loves father or mother more than me is not worthy of me; and he who loves son or daughter more than me is not worthy of me.* 38*And he who does not take up his cross and follow me is not worthy of me."*

The reader who has pondered well the preceding verses (34–36) will also be able to understand these words. The previous text spoke of God and the decision for him. Here, however, it is Jesus himself before whom and for whom the disciple has to make his decision. He is the way which leads to God. Or to put it another way: in the decision for him is realized the decision for God. Before this, every other earthly tie, even the bonds between father and mother and their own children, must yield. Not that parents or children are not to be loved, preciscly the opposite is true. Whoever follows Christ totally will become free in a new way for love of his fellow men and his family. But that is a new, " supernatural " love which is able to love the neighbor in God and for the sake of God. Before the disciple becomes capable of this, he must have decided totally for Christ.

Any other is not worthy of him. Nothing is gained by a divided heart and a decision that goes only halfway. God does not then receive his due which is total dedication, nor does Jesus receive his due which is to follow him unconditionally, nor does the disciple gain himself the fulfillment of his life. Only he who has given his heart away receives it back anew, filled with the divine force of love.

The next saying makes this clearer. " He who does not take up his cross and follow me." The rejection of self and dedication to God have something external to be measured by. There is a boundary in life against which can be seen whether dedication is the act of the whole will. This boundary is death. He who in his daring option for God has also included the possible giving of his life has made a radical decision. To " take up his cross " is a metaphorical expression for the readiness to die. The movement away from me—unto God finds its completion in this. Only when the disciple has taken this supreme offering into account and deliberately assented to it, is he really in the following of Christ and so worthy of the Master. It is not asked of every disciple that he give proof of this readiness by actually suffering death. Only certain chosen ones are led by God along this way as a sign to others. But all dedication—and that is the theme of our lives—has something in it of this dying. Are we ready for it or not? That is the infallible criterion of the sincerity of our hearts.

39" *He who has found his life shall lose it, and he who loses his life for my sake shall find it.*"

The soul is not spoken of here in opposition to the body. This distinction had no great meaning in the Old Testament. Under the word life we are to understand the unity of body and soul. For the Jew, life was the supreme good and the fulfillment of all desires was most fully expressed in this word. His yearnings are satisfied when he has his whole life, enduringly and indestructibly, in overflowing richness and blessed possession.

This deep yearning implanted in man by God himself seems to be sharply denied by Jesus' words: " He who has found his life shall lose it!" By this he means that man thinks he has already come to rest here and may already enjoy the possession of life. His striving has closed in on itself and become avarice; he does not wish to go beyond himself, and in the last resort seeks only himself. The yearning is the same and its fulfillment also seems to be the same, but the routes take exactly opposite directions. No doubt life is to be won, and we are called thereto. But it is only won when we lose it.

" He who loses it for my sake "—that may well mean actual martyrdom for Jesus. Then eternal life will be bestowed for the earthly life that has been given up. We shall find what we have really sought. But it is still a fundamental law in the life of the disciple, even if he is not called to give the supreme proof. Each one must first abandon his life and not try to attain it for himself in egoistic desire. The law is to go out of oneself, to strive for something beyond oneself; though not by a sort of drill in the sense of certain methods of emptying of desire. For that would be ultimately a sort of egoism which seeks one's own independence from the passions of each day and the assaults of instinct, and so only a higher form of human perfection. Jesus means what rang out again and again throughout the Sermon on the Mount: that man's losing himself must be directed towards God and into God. He who does that wins full life, ultimately God's own life.

Thus this saying is not really gloomy, but optimistic. Even here on earth one can experience in grace that every single act of losing oneself in dedication to God (in practice, mostly to the neighbor) increases life. This life is much richer than any earthly life. It is joy, inner peace, security in God, love. Thus the truth is exactly the opposite of what Goethe's Faust says: " So I go stumbling from desires to delights, and in delights I languish for desires." Rather, we go from death to life, and in life we go to ever greater fullness—through death itself. Jesus says: " I am come that they may have life, and have it in all fullness " (Jn. 10:10).

Mission and Reward (10:40–42)

[40]" He that receives you, receives me; and he that receives me, receives him that sent me."

This first saying explicates what the rabbis already taught as the rule: a man's messenger is like the man himself. But Jesus here speaks not of one but of two missions which are mysteriously interlocked in their action. Jesus himself has been sent by the Father, and he in turn sends out the apostles. A movement which starts from the Father reaches down to the envoys of Jesus. Their mission is a divine event. Men's reactions to them —in accepting or refusing, in faith or disbelief—are men's reactions to Jesus and to the Father. We cannot appeal to God or Christ against the envoys. God comes down into the messengers; he veils himself in human word and work. Faith is only true when it no longer takes scandal at the brittle forms of human action; only then is it surely directed to God and perfected in obedience.

[41]" *He who receives a prophet in the name of a prophet will receive the reward of a prophet; and he who receives a just man in the name of the just will receive the reward of a just man.* [42]*And whoever gives one of these little ones even a glass of water in the name of a disciple, truly, I tell you, he will not lose his reward.*"

Three community groups are named together here. The prophets are specially called men of God who teach the faith from their own knowledge and experience, though they have not a place in the official hierarchy like an apostle, a disciple of the apostles, an elder or overseer. The just are those who have proved themselves in the community by the good example of their lives, by a faith active in love. They have no official rank nor have they a charismatic mission to teach, like the prophets, but they have their importance as models for practical life. The third group are the little ones. These are simple disciples of Jesus who have no leading part in the Christian communities. The miracle of faith is especially great in them since they apparently bring with them none of the conditions which are outwardly favorable: culture, high rank, power, and influence. They should be particularly dear to the community and cherished by it with watchful care.

In the first two cases the reward is meted out exactly. It is hard to say what we are to understand by the reward of a prophet or the reward of the just. The basic thought of v. 40 is no doubt still at work here, so that we may say: " A man's messenger is like the man himself." And that now means that whoever receives the wandering prophet as guest in his house is thereby placed on the same footing as the prophet and receives the reward which is granted to the prophet. So too with the just. That the little ones are treasured most especially is expressed by the fact that even the tiniest thing done for them does not go unnoticed. For the " little one " does not enter the house as a minor element, as an unimportant contemporary to whom one does not have to pay much attention, but as a disciple. It is " in the name of a disciple " that one does good to him, perhaps no more than giving him a cup of water. Because he has the high dignity of a disciple Jesus himself comes along with him, and therefore the reward. Such words explain how hospitality is so highly treasured in the Christian church: if a brother or a priest comes to the house, we welcome him not just out of politeness, but in faith, like Jesus.

With these words the instruction of the disciples comes to an end. In the whole section the doctrine is concerned with the call and the mission of the disciple to the world. And here too, the matter of the discourse comes to a climax. All that went before receives new light from these last phrases. Mission and mandate, doctrine and miracle, persecution and profession of faith, endurance and death—all this makes the messenger like the one who sent him, the apostles like Jesus. This remains true today, since the mission of Jesus is handed on further through the apostles to the bishops, to their fellow workers, to all the faithful. It is always the Lord who sends them: in the course of history by means of the mandate once given (the succession of pope and bishops), and by means of an immediate call to the individual here and now. It is always true that " He who hears you, hears me " (Lk. 10:16).

The Conclusion (11:1)

¹And it came to pass when Jesus had completed instructing his disciples, that he went on from that place to teach and preach in their cities.

Once more, as at the end of the Sermon on the Mount, the evangelist rounds off the discourse with a sort of formula. The word " instructing " is remarkable and it occurs only here in this gospel. Matthew wishes again to insist that we are concerned in this discourse especially with an official administrative instruction from the Lord. For all time to come, it remains the fundamental document of the apostolic mission and life.

Between Faith and Unbelief (11:2—12:45)

After the discourse on discipleship comes a long section about the work of Jesus. This time only a few miracles are included. The principal object of the section is to present the conflicts between Jesus and his opponents. All the episodes contribute to this theme: the reaction for or against Jesus, the crisis in his work, the embittered enmity on the part of official Judaism. The first main portion deals with John the Baptist (11:2-19). The second part puts before us two long statements of Jesus which throw light on the contrasts (11:20-30). The third part contains new charges brought by Jesus' opponents on the occasion of particular happenings (12:1-45).

Jesus and the Baptist (11:2-19)

THE BAPTIST'S INQUIRY (11:2-6)

²But when John heard in prison of the works of the Messiah, he sent his disciples ³to ask: " Are you he that is to come, or are we to wait for another?" ⁴And Jesus answered them and said: " Go and recount to John what you hear and see: ⁵Blind men see and lame men walk, lepers are cleansed and deaf men hear, dead men arise and poor men are brought good news. ⁶And blessed is he that does not take offence at me."

Since 4:12 we have heard no more about John. He is in prison. The immediate circumstances which brought him there will be told only later (14:3-12). The first sentence really anticipates the answer since it mentions the " works of the Messiah." For the Messiah is of course " he who is to come." " But he who comes after me is stronger than I " (3:11). Now doubts arise in his mind as to whether Jesus really is he " who holds the winnowing shovel already in his hand " (3:12) and none other. The question which the Baptist causes to be put by his disciples is a genuine question and is meant seriously. Matthew explains it by the fact that John is in fact in prison and so cut off from the outer world.

He has indeed heard of the works but he does not know how to interpret them. Or had he expected a quite different set of works, a spontaneous movement of the people, a mighty judgment on the enemies of God? The whirlwind of judgment, the first gusts of which had shaken John himself, had not come.

Jesus does not answer directly with a declaration about his own person. He could have answered, as before the High Priest, with a clear yes. But he still evades it at the moment, and shows John the way which the disciples and all of us must go: to see signs and interpret them rightly, to see the works that Jesus does and understand them as works of the Messiah. This is the way of faith which takes the visible effect as its starting point and leads to knowledge of Jesus. It is the way from darkness to light, from sign to reality.

He who comprehends the works rightly, and above all, sees them as connected together, cannot be a prey to doubt. Jesus himself builds the bridge to faith because the enumeration, " Blind see . . ." etc., is closely connected with the promise of the prophet Isaiah (Is. 35 : 5f.; 61 : 1). The Spirit who has anointed the elect made him capable of all these glorious deeds. We may not stand still at any one of them, we may not look at certain wonders and disregard others, we may not only listen to the words and ignore the works. The correct picture is given only when all are taken together. Jesus is in fact not only a popular preacher and wonder worker. And he has not only performed healings like a doctor, he has also raised the dead. All this taken together gives us to understand that here the Anointed of God, whom Isaiah saw, is at work. The church, too, is only recognized as a sign from God when all its notes are seen together: its unity, holiness, universality (catholicity), and its historic continuity with its origin (apostolicity).

THE TESTIMONY OF JESUS TO THE BAPTIST (11:7-15)

There is no one of whom Jesus has spoken so much as the Baptist. The earnest speech, with brief questions following each other like hammerblows, shows us Jesus once more as a great prophetic speaker. These words are not just a revelation about the significance of John in the process of salvation. They are also a testimony to the deep impression which the Baptist, even as a man, had left on Jesus.

⁷But when they went away Jesus began to speak to the crowds about John: " Why did you go out to the desert? To see a reed shaken by the wind? ⁸Or why did you go out? To see a man clothed in soft garments? Behold, they who wear soft garments live in the palaces of the kings. ⁹Or why did you go out? To see a prophet? Yes, I tell you, more than a prophet."

Jesus uses his questions to bring the people to think over what they sought when they marched in throngs to the Jordan. The great surge seems to have ebbed away. But the memory was deeply engraved in all of them. Jesus points once more with his questions to the picture of the austere figure. He was not like a reed which is moved to and fro by the wind. He was not one who waited to see which way the wind was blowing, upholding one view today, another tomorrow. He delivered his message straightforwardly and without disguising it, and addressed himself to each man's conscience no matter what his rank, even the king. He did not cut a figure in fine clothes of soft material, no, such are to be found in the palaces of the great, the rich, and the mighty. John stood before them like a wild, gnarled oak tree.

They looked for a prophet and they found one. The interrupted chain of prophets was linked up again in his person. In the last resort, that was what drew men out to him: God was speaking once more through the prophetic word which had moved Israel for centuries. The people knew all this, and the words of Jesus must have found a strong echo in their hearts. But now he goes on to say more.

John is more than a prophet. He is not merely God's sounding box, the intermediary of his message to the people. He is also in himself a bearer of salvation, a salvific figure. Not by his own personality or by his ascetic life, but because from the very start his work is greater than that of the other prophets. It lends him his unique significance. He alone was called to prepare the people and to lead them to one that was stronger than he and was to come after him (3:11).

¹⁰" *This is he of whom it is written: ' Behold, I send my messenger before you, who shall prepare the way before you '.*"

The messianic preaching of the Baptist and his immediate proximity to Jesus make him the precursor. Isaiah had already spoken of the preparation of the way: God leads his people back in jubilation out of captivity and is to march along a straight and level way in doing so. It leads from slavery to freedom (Is. 40:4f.; Mt. 3:3). The prophet Malachi says more. He is concerned with the way of God to his people. But no longer to free them from the Babylonian captivity, it is to redeem them at the end of time. God himself will come. A herald goes before him: " Behold, I am sending my messenger before you, who shall prepare the way before you " (Mal. 3:1). These prophetic words give the light in which the figure of the Baptist is to be seen as part of God's plan of salvation. Here Jesus himself sees him in that light. In doing so he testifies indirectly that he himself is the Messiah of the end of time, for whom John has built the way.

[11]" Truly, I tell you: among those that have been born of woman, none greater has arisen than John the Baptist; but the least in the kingdom of heaven is greater than he."

More than a prophet—that means something different. John is not merely a great figure in his office of preparing the way. He is also a great figure as a man: there is no greater among those born of woman. An astonishing saying! It has the air of being thrown in as a piece of hyperbole, and yet it is still meant as personal praise of this man. It raises John above the ranks of his contemporaries and, indeed, above the great host of men of God in the past.

"Among those who are born of woman" is of itself merely a ceremonious turn of speech such as the Oriental loves. But when Jesus uses it, it also has overtones of his own mysterious origin. He too is born of a woman, but only " according to the flesh " (Rom. 1:3). His origin as God-man is in a sphere beyond that of human generation. He is " born of God."

The next saying adds a restriction to what has just been said. Great as John the Baptist is, he cannot compare to one in heaven. " The least in the kingdom of heaven is greater than he." The new age has already begun, the kingship of God is advancing along its way. Whoever lives in this period is still greater than anyone who lived before, greater even than the Baptist. The thought is novel. Alongside the high place accorded to John comes the evaluation of the new age, the epoch of the kingship of God. The man of this age, the man in grace, the redeemed man, stands on a higher level. Old and new are related to each other as the image to the reality.

[12]" But from the days of John the Baptist until now, the kingdom

of heaven suffers violence, and violent men rob it. [12]*For all prophets and the law have prophesied up to John."*

The question arises of where the Baptist then stands in the history of salvation? He is, after all, a transitional figure, half in shadow, half in light, at once he who foretells the future and already prepares it. Is he outside or inside the section which divides the two periods? Up to this we have heard sayings which would allow us to suspect both. John comes before the cleavage since the least in the kingdom of heaven is greater than he. But he could also come after it, since he is more than a prophet as the precursor of the Messiah. The evangelist does not develop any further here the thought that John is less than a member of the kingdom of heaven. He takes up the other, namely, that John is included in the new age.

From the days of John the Baptist on—that means, starting with him, his coming forward, his preaching. From this moment on, the kingdom of heaven is present, for it is being hard pressed. Here we learn of the darker side of the arrival of the kingship. Hitherto we had heard almost only of the lightsome side, of its victorious advance, of its healing and lifegiving powerfulness. But the other side had been shown by the many attacks of the opponents, the most vicious of which was the charge that Jesus was working in league with the devil. Fierce resistance is being offered to the kingship. Its progress is being hindered, and indeed violently held up. And that ultimately means that God is being hindered in his course and his work brought to naught.

Jesus sees this so vividly that he speaks of violent men, who try to rob the kingship. It is not merely to be weakened and hindered in its course, it is actually to be rendered harmless. This is a dark saying. We can gain perhaps some little help for the

understanding of the difficult saying from the story of the temptation. There, too, Satan aims at nothing less than everything;
he tries to seize the lordship for himself and to rob it. As Jesus'
work goes on, he disguises himself behind all the adversaries,
and tries in various ways to contest God's lordship and install
his own in its place. Once more we get a glimpse into the
abysmal depths which these powers are constantly stirring up.

The truth about John, however, is that from his time on the
kingdom of heaven is somehow there, above all, through what
Jesus does and preaches. The law and the prophets reached as
far as John. Their task was to lead to, to indicate beforehand,
what was to come. But with the Baptist what was to come has
already begun. The time of prophecy is past, the time of fulfillment is there.

[14]" *And if you are willing to accept it, this is Elijah, who is to
come.* [15]*He that has ears to hear, let him hear."*

We have heard that John is the precursor, as Malachi said
(11 : 10). In the same prophecy a few verses later there is another
announcement: " Behold, I send to you the prophet Elijah, before
the great and terrible day of the Lord comes " (Mal. 3 : 23).
According to the belief of the times, Elijah was to come before the
Messiah, to prepare for his arrival. Here both predictions are com-
bined. The nameless messenger of Malachi 3 : 1 is the Elijah of
3 : 23. And John the Baptist is both together! Of course one is not
to think that Elijah appeared bodily in John, that the Baptist was
a sort of incarnation of Elijah. But he goes before Jesus " in the
spirit and the power of Elijah " (Lk. 1 : 17).

If Jesus was the real Messiah, then one should have also been
able to point to his precursor. Since the Jews said that Jesus could

not be the Messiah because after all Elijah did not appear, it had to be possible to say to them: Elijah was already there. It was John, but you did not recognize him. This can only be grasped by faith as the last phrase shows: " He that has ears to hear, let him hear." Only one who opens his ears and is ready to understand correctly and take to heart what he has heard can also recognize what is said here. So too with all the mysteries of faith: there are helpful indications, bridges that God has built. But the actual acceptance is a matter of our own ready will to believe.

CHARGES AGAINST "THIS GENERATION" (11:16-19)

16" But to whom shall I compare this generation? It is like children who sit in the marketplace and cry out to the others: 17' We have piped for you, and you have not danced. We have mourned, and you have not beaten your breasts.' "

The theme continues to treat John the Baptist and his place in the act of salvation. But now it takes the form of a word of blame for this generation which is moody and fickle, indeed, quite unpredictable, like children who play in the street. One group of them strikes up a gay tune, but the others are not interested. So they try a melancholy air, a funeral march, but again the others will not join in. They find everything wrong, they are bad-tempered spoilsports. How is it with you, with this generation, the contemporaries of John and Jesus? Exactly as with these children, only that here what is at stake is not a game, but life.

18" For John came, ate nothing and drank nothing—and they said: ' He has a demon.' 19ªThe Son of Man came, ate and drank

—and they said: ' Look, a glutton and a drunkard, a friend of tax gatherers and sinners! ' "

John did not suit them because he lived a life of strict penance. So they said, " He has a demon." He did not suit them and he could not please them; he did not dance to their tune, and so without more ado they put the blame for his failure on him: " He is mad." They said the same sort of thing about Jesus himself. It is the simplest way of shirking the call: to trace back to the devil the work wrought by God.

Then came Jesus who did not lead the austere life of an ascetic. He brought the time of joy, the time of fullness during which there was to be no fasting (9:14f.). He took pity on the outcasts and had no misgivings about dining with tax collectors and sinners (9:10–12). This now they felt to be too worldly. So they make hateful and insulting reproaches against him which in no place in the gospels find such crude expression as here. Is there anyone who will please you? Is there anyone at all that you will believe?

[19b]*" And wisdom is justified by her works."*

But the judgment of men is wrong, and it leaves them both unscathed. For in both of them, Jesus and John, divine wisdom was at work. She made the latter the dour preacher of penance, and the former the bringer of joy and the heavenly bridegroom. What both have done are works of divine wisdom, thought out in the depths of God and wrought in the Holy Spirit. He who has ears to hear and eyes to see, he who has a sense and feeling for the supernatural will be able to recognize the divine character of the works. Thus divine wisdom will be justified if men are found who believe in the works. In face of such justification, all human misinterpretation is silenced. Everything that God does is ultimately accessible only to the eyes of faith. But whoever sees with the eyes of faith can recognize everywhere, even in the visible figure of the church, the work of divine wisdom. We must strive hard—like the contemporaries of the Baptist and of Jesus—to look at things in this supernatural way, and so recognize the invisible God and the works of his wisdom in the outward sensible signs.

Judgment and Salvation (11:20–30)

The Woes upon the Cities of Galilee (11:20–24)

²⁰Then he began to upbraid the cities in which most of his miracles had been done because they had not been converted.

Jesus' discourse works up to a menacing word of doom. It is not a game as with the children in the marketplace, it is a matter of life and death. The moody fickleness of the people is in the last resort just lack of faith, the refusal of God. Even though they had not believed Jesus' words, still, his works should have convinced them. Even such cities as had seen Jesus working many miracles within their walls had not been converted. The cities which the Lord names here, Chorozin, Bethsaida, and Capernaum are all in Galilee, on the shore of Lake Genesareth.

²¹" Woe to you, Chorozin! Woe to you, Bethsaida! For if the wonders that have been done in you had been done in Tyre and Sidon, they would have long since been converted in sackcloth and ashes. ²²But I tell you: It will be more bearable for Tyre and Sidon on the day of judgment than for you. ²³And you, Capernaum, shall you perhaps be exalted to heaven? You shall be hurled down to hell! For if the wonders that have been done in you had been done in Sodom, it would be standing till this very day. ²⁴But I tell you: It will be more bearable for the land of Sodom on the day of judgment than for you."

" Woe to you "—that is the cry of doom, the opposite of the prophetic " Blessed are you!" The " Woe!" both threatens disaster and brings it effectively on the scene, just as the beatitude already gives reality to salvation as it is uttered. There are in the scriptures some typical examples of unrepentant cities: the heathen cities of Tyre and Sidon in the north of Palestine, proverbial in the prophets as examples of boastful arrogance and luxurious riches; Sodom and Gomorrha, the cities of licentiousness and vice, which were erased from the face of the earth. As the heathen centurion found his way to faith, so too the heathen cities would certainly have been converted if they had seen the miracles of Jesus. And Sodom would certainly have been standing until that day if it had witnessed the glorious demonstrations of Jesus' might.

That will all be made clear on the day of judgment. These cities will then be better treated than the places where Jesus worked. For they have rejected the offer of grace and have wasted the time of decision. The offer had been made to all, to the whole population of a city. Jesus sees all the inhabitants linked together in a common destiny. In the personal encounter it is, of course, always the individual he calls and who comes to faith. But all are there for each other and responsible for each other. When God's kingship arrives it is a public, indeed a political event which concerns all. God can give a community, a city, a nation, the benefit of a sign. He can make an offer that obliges all. This has happened again and again down to our own days. The thing is to be sharp of hearing when the call to repent goes forth.

THE REVELATION OF SALVATION (11:25–27)

There follow two important sayings of Jesus about the majesty of God. The evangelist makes them stand out by the introduction " at that time." The first saying is an outburst of praise for the greatness of God who has revealed himself to the little ones and to the " minors " as to no one else (11:25f.). The second saying grants us a deep insight into the innermost mystery of Jesus (11:27).

25At that time Jesus said: " I praise you, Father, Lord of heaven and earth, for you have hidden this from the wise and prudent and revealed it to the children. 26Yes, Father, so was your good pleasure."

This is the only place in the gospel where we find the solemn address: " Father, Lord of heaven and earth." Up to this Jesus spoke of the Father, of his or our Father, in the easy, familiar tones which this form of address has. Here however it is said expressly that the Father is also the almighty Creator and Lord of the world. He is the God who " in the beginning created " (Gen. 1:1) heaven and earth. Beside him there is no God. All that still exists in the whole world is subject to him as the supreme Lord.

The solemn title is significant here because it is what allows us to appreciate properly the words which follow. For this great God who sustains all things has bestowed his revelation on the simple. He has not chosen for it the people who are wise and understanding, the prudent and the learned. Jesus does not say what God has made known, but only " this." From the gospel, as far as we have read up to now, we know that this means the whole message of Jesus in his miracles and in his words. It was to the poor in spirit that Jesus called out his first " Blessed " (5 : 3); it was the humble folk, the despised and outcast, and above all the unlearned whom Jesus sought out. He called them to be his disciples; such were the people who believed in him and prayed for his miracles—like the woman who suffered from the flow of blood or the two blind men. It seems almost as though God had a preference, even a sort of weakness, for those who do not count for anything in the world.

But the wise and prudent go away empty-handed. The mystery of God is concealed from them so that they do not see and recognize it; they do not hear and believe it. As in the Old Testament, so too the acceptance or refusal is here ascribed to God alone. It is he who opens the heart, or again, as with Pharaoh, hardens the heart. But that does not happen without man's own decision. God's action is his answer to men's hearts, when they have already barred themselves and become impenetrable to God's word. Although by reason of their gifted minds, their knowledge and their insight, they should have been particularly fitted to understand the speech of God, they close their minds to it and it remains hidden from them. Jesus must have been thinking especially of the doctors of the scribes. They used their intelligence to develop a closed view of God and the world; they were unready to hear and learn anything new. They imagine they know everything about God and that they possess the correct doctrine. Ever since the tempter suggested to Eve that her and Adam's eyes would be opened and they would be like God if they ate of the tree of knowledge, this has been the eternal temptation of the human spirit.

Thus God can only count on the simple who throw open their hearts and believe unpretentiously. What a strange reversal of the order of things! And yet God chooses this way because they are the only ones whom his message can reach. This way corresponds to his will; it is his good pleasure. How much of the world becomes understandable when we keep these words before our mind!

[27]" *All things have been delivered over to me by my Father and no one knows the Son but the Father, and no one knows the Father but the Son, and he to whom the Son wills to reveal him.*"

This saying is concerned with knowledge. This is not sheer intellectual knowledge. In the Bible " to know " means far more than that. The image of the tree of knowledge in the garden of Eden designates an all-embracing knowledge, an immediate insight into the reasons and causes of things. To know means further, a familiarity with something, taking it to oneself with understanding. Will, affection, and understanding all form part of the knowledge in the same way. Hence scripture can talk of the deepest meeting of man and woman in marriage as " knowing." When God knows man he penetrates him entirely with his Spirit and enfolds him at the same time with his loving affection. There, to know and to love are one.

Jesus says: " No one knows the Son but the Father," the same Father who has just been praised as Lord of heaven and earth (11:25). He himself is the Son because he calls God " his Father." Here we learn for the first time of this most profound relation between God and him who here speaks as a man among men. The images of " Father " and " Son " taken from our natural experience become vehicles of the mystery in God. There is only one who embraces the Son totally in loving knowledge: and that is the Father.

Still more astonishing is the inversion: " And no one knows the Father but the Son." Hitherto Jesus had always spoken of God in a reverent manner and he goes on doing so. But in the depths of his being he is like the Father; he too knows him fully and completely. Indeed, there was and is no one else in the world who has such knowledge. Jesus is God. This is the only place in the synoptic gospels in which the divine Sonship of the Messiah is so clearly expressed. The saying stands there alone and lofty. It grants us, as through a rift in the clouds, a glimpse into the depth of the mystery of God. Reverently, and like a " little one " must we accept it.

But the Son of God does not possess this knowledge only on his own behalf, he is to impart it to others. It is his mission to reveal the kingship of God. What has just been said of God is also the work of the Son: " And to whom the Son wills to reveal it." That has been given into his hand since the Father has " delivered all things " to him. So in the end it seems to be the same thing whether anything be attributed to the Father or the Son. If the Father has given everything into his hands, the whole revelation, then the Son may freely dispose of it and impart it to whom he wills. And in spite of this, it remains always the word and work of the Father. For they are one in their mutual knowledge and love. What Jesus speaks, even of himself, comes always as a gift out of the depths of God to us. It is not easy to come to terms with this thought. The scandal which the Jews then took still dogs our footsteps. How can a human being speak in this way? Is not this the son of the carpenter? If one approaches it with a critical intelligence, as the opponents already did in early Christian times, then one grasps nothing at all. One understands as little as " this generation " which could make no headway at all, either with John or with Jesus. Only the open-hearted readiness of a " little one," not the exorbitant self-assurance of the wise and prudent, can succeed here. " He who does not receive the kingship of God like a child, cannot enter therein " (Mk. 10:15).

THE MILD YOKE (11:28–30)

[28]" *Come to me all you who are laboring and heavy burdened, and I will refresh you.* [29]*Take my yoke upon you and learn of me, for I am meek and humble of heart and you shall find rest for your souls.* [30]*For my yoke is easy and my burden is light.*"

Jesus has once more the same men in mind to whom all his affection was inclined: the poor and hungry, the ignorant and simple, the sick and sighing. They have always pressed round him, to bring him their sick, to listen to his word, indeed just to try and touch even the tassel on his robe. And he too had always gone to them of his own accord and he had eaten with the outcasts. Now he calls them all to him and promises them that he will refresh them. They are like sheep without shepherds, dispersed and exhausted. They are burdened and they groan under the yoke. This is the load of their oppressed and toilsome lives, but above all, the load of an intolerable interpretation of the law. This double burden leaves them tired and heavy. But Jesus will make them joyful and light of step.

The doctors of the law impose on them the hard and galling yoke of the law's regulations as a peasant loads a beast of burden. They make of the law which had, after all, been given for the sake of salvation and life (Ezek. 20 : 13), an unbearable load of hundreds of particular regulations. No one could keep them all, and the scribes themselves were not equal to it. Jesus has an easy yoke, that is, one that fits well. Though he makes difficult demands and teaches the law in a far more radical fashion (the Sermon on the Mount), still, this yoke of Jesus is of benefit to man. It does not fret and gall him; and man himself does not chafe against it until blood comes. " His commandments are not heavy " (1 Jn 5 : 3)—because they are simple and contain only two demands: self-devotion and love.

Nevertheless, the will of God is a yoke and a burden. But they become light if we do one thing: "Learn of me!" Jesus too bears both; his mission is a yoke and a burden for him. But he has accepted it as humble servant of God. He has made himself lowly, and he performs in full submissiveness all that God has enjoined upon him. He makes himself the servant of all. Although the Father has delivered all to him he has become as lowly as the meanest slave.

If the yoke of the new teaching is thus accepted, the promise will be fulfilled: " And you shall find rest for your souls." This is not the sleepy calm of well-to-do comfort, or the lazy peace that has settled down to co-exist with evil (Jesus has uttered the word about the sword! [10 : 34]). Jesus promises refreshment for the tiresome burden of everyday life, for the accomplishment of the will of God in all things, great and small. He whose life is dedicated to God and who constantly practices charity will be inwardly glad and happy. Our faith must never become an oppressive weight, a yoke against which one chafes until one is sore. If so, it would certainly not be genuine. But if one really tries to keep his commandments, the yoke of Jesus will be an unfailing source of consolation and joyful abandonment. One should surely be able to recognize the disciples of Jesus by this sign.

True or False Observance of the Sabbath (12:1–21)

The discussion is continued. The two following episodes deal with the proper understanding of the sabbath as Jesus develops it in his defense. We hear first of the disciples' plucking ears of corn on the sabbath (12:1–8), and then of the healing of a sufferer on the sabbath (12:9–14). A section in the form of a résumé concludes this passage (12:15–21).

PLUCKING EARS OF CORN ON THE SABBATH (12:1–8)

¹*At that time, Jesus was going through the fields of corn on the sabbath. But his disciples were hungry and began to pluck ears of corn and to eat them.* ²*But the Pharisees saw it and said to him: " See, your disciples are doing what one is forbidden to do on the sabbath."* ³*And he said to them: " Have you not read what David did when he and his companions were hungry?* ⁴*How he went into the House of God and ate the bread of the Presence which he and his companions were not allowed to eat, but only the priests?"*

Jesus gives his opponents new grounds for complaint. One sabbath day, as his disciples were on the road, they happened to pluck some ears of corn and eat the grain to still their hunger. This was expressly permitted by the law if the corn was eaten on the spot, and immemorial custom had sanctioned it. "If you come into your neighbor's corn field, you may break off some ears with your hand; but you may not swing the sickle upon the corn of your neighbor " (Deut. 23:25). The Pharisees blamed Jesus only because he permitted it on the sabbath without interfering. According to their strict interpretation, even quite trifling activities came under the prohibition of sabbath work. One was allowed to walk only a certain distance and to perform only the manual works necessary for life. Even to pluck and rub the grains was considered forbidden work!

Jesus defends himself in a rather long speech, which is built up by stages as argument is added to argument. There are four independent thoughts which serve first of all to demonstrate that Jesus has right on his side and is not violating the law of God. His final proof and indeed the decisive counter argument presupposes, however, that faith in the authority of Jesus is already there: " For the Son of Man is Lord of the sabbath." Here, as earlier on the question of fasting, Jesus speaks from the viewpoint of his unique mission. In the time of the messianic marriage feast, there is no reason to fast. The sabbath too, the interpretation of the sabbath law and the manner of celebrating it are all submitted to Jesus as Lord. Relying on such sayings, the ancient Christians could well dare to celebrate the sabbath in their own way, and finally even to replace it by the celebration of the first day of the week. This goes back to the authority of the *Kyrios* which he transmitted to the apostles.

In the scripture itself, however, there are examples of the sabbath's being broken. The first deals with David, the exemplary king, to whose way of acting one could rightly appeal. While flying from Saul, David made the priest Abimeleck give him and his companions the sacred show breads which were kept in the holy tent at Nob (1 Sam. 21 : 1–7). These should have been eaten only by the priests. David disregarded this because the liturgical law was not as important to him as the duty of sustaining life. For Jesus, the sabbath laws are on the same footing as this regulation about the show bread! What David did, did not take place on the sabbath. The comparison ultimately lies in the transgression of a legal prescription; in special cases, such a commandment may be transgressed.

⁵" Or have you not read in the law that on the sabbath the priests in the temple profane the sabbath and are guiltless? ⁶But I tell you, here is more than the temple."

The second example is even stronger. The priests who are engaged in the temple do all sorts of manual labour on the sabbath while preparing and slaughtering the victims, collecting offerings, and purifying vessels. All this is not just permitted as an exception, but is expressly commanded in the law. They do it and remain without guilt. How much more must this freedom be now in force since here there is " more than the temple." This is a tremendous saying. Israel knows no greater sanctuary than the temple, which is the guarantee of the presence of God. In the legal charges brought against Jesus a saying opposed to the holiness of the temple was to play an important role (26 : 61; see Acts 7 : 47–50). In the temple only the nearness of God is guaranteed. But in Jesus God is visibly present. He dwells among us; God has become man. This dignity is of course infinitely greater than that of the house of wood and stone.

⁷" If you had understood what this means: ' Mercy is what I

want and not sacrifice,' then you would not have condemned the innocent. ⁸For the Son of Man is Lord of the sabbath."

The third argument is one that we have already met: the saying of the prophet Hosea: " Mercy is what I want and not sacrifice " (9 : 13). Jesus upholds once more the proper order of values as the prophets before him had been tireless in doing. God desires the heart, he wants obedience and confidence, kindness and true justice. Only when man has achieved this are his sacrifices also pleasing to God. But we may never absolve ourselves from our first duty by dint of painstaking observance of ritual prescriptions and the minute fulfillment of liturgical regulations. When we give God the one without the other we fail to do his will.

The proofs given by Jesus go far beyond their occasion. He takes up the question of the true understanding of the law of God, and especially its cultic regulations. Jesus does not say that the sabbath laws have been abolished, but they are given a new meaning. There are higher duties than these and they are urged more strongly by God. Above all, once Jesus himself has appeared, a new situation has been created. In him there is something absolutely greater than the temple and its worship. It is the rosy dawn of a new era in which the true adorers of God will worship him no longer in the temple, but " in the Spirit and truth " (Jn. 4 : 23). The order of things set up by Jesus remains valid also for us: first obedience and mercy, then the fulfillment of cultic prescriptions. It is true that the worship of God in the new covenant has an incomparable dignity since it is offered by the High Priest Jesus. But everywhere the danger still threatens of legalistic narrow-mindedness and of excessive multiplication of rites and rubrics overshadowing the living service of the heart.

THE HEALING OF A WITHERED HAND ON THE SABBATH (12:9–14)

*⁹And he went on farther from there and entered their synagogue.
¹⁰And behold, there was a man there with a withered hand. They
questioned him and said: " Is it permitted to heal on the sabbath?"—so as to be able to accuse him. ¹¹But he said to them:
" Which of you who has one sheep will not seize it and draw
it out if it falls into a pit on the sabbath? ¹²How much more is
a man worth than a sheep! Thus it is permitted to do good on
the sabbath." ¹³Then he said to the man: " Stretch out your
hand!" And he stretched it out, and it was restored, healthy like
the other. ¹⁴But the Pharisees went out and made a resolution
about him, that they would kill him.*

A second conflict on the sabbath—and what is more, in a synagogue. This time his opponents are beforehand with their attack
when they ask is it permitted to heal on the sabbath. The scribes
themselves maintained various opinions on the subject, many
taking a magnanimous view, many others a narrow-minded one.
But Jesus is not asked to choose between these views, but to say
whether any healing was allowed at all.

The Lord answers first with an example. The case of the sheep
which he propounds would have been also deemed permissible in
certain circumstances according to many opinions upheld in the
schools. But Jesus does not recount the example to assert and
defend an opinion of the scribes. Rather, he speaks from the
standpoint of sound human intelligence. Every reasonable man
will act like the peasant in question. It will occur to nobody to
let the sheep perish miserably for the sake of the sabbath, especially since it is the peasant's only sheep and so represents something of high value to him.

But now comes the deduction. A man is worth much more than a sheep. If he has an accident, others will help him at once, even if it is the sabbath. But the man with the withered hand has not in fact fallen into a pit; he is in no immediate danger of his life. Jesus could have healed him just as well the next day! But he wants to answer the question on the grounds of principle, just as he has been questioned on a matter of principle. He does so with a significant shift of position. His opponents ask him whether one may heal. He answers that one may do good. That therefore is what is at stake. The measure of what is permitted or not is not to be gauged by the character of the work alone, but also by the intention of this work. Here it is something good, beneficial, and hence, from the start, well-pleasing to God. Here too, Jesus calls us to reconsider. The fixed ideas of a formal legalistic thinking must be replaced by a humane form of thought which is determined by moral intentions and values. There is always sense and meaning in doing good. We must always do it spontaneously and heartily, without pondering timorously or reassuring ourselves carefully.

The sick man is healed. But according to the ideas of his opponents Jesus breaks the law. And not only that, he maintains a new doctrine and thereby puts himself outside the pale of tradition. This makes them so angry that they already decree his death. The announcement of the murderous plan of the enemies rings out like a clap of thunder. All is clear. It is not a matter of holding one opinion or another, of interpreting the scripture in a strict or liberal manner, it is a matter of fundamental hostility. What is new in Jesus has for them no connection with the old. It is a revolution which must be suppressed if the foundations of their faith are to remain unshaken. Thus they may think, and really believe, that they are right—although all the right of

God is on the side of Jesus. But blinded by their rigid legalism, they cannot see.

THE SERVANT OF GOD (12:15–21)

[15]But when Jesus learned of this, he withdrew from there. And many followed him, and he healed them all. [16]And he commanded them not to make him known . . .

Matthew takes up a thought which is often expressed by Mark, that the Lord commanded silence about his miracles and the mystery of his person. This command of silence receives here a special character on account of the plan to kill him which has just been mentioned (12 : 14). It looks as if Jesus was evading his opponents and going into hiding. Hence he must not be made known. It is true that he continues his acts of healing, but not in order that they may be widely spoken of. The time seems to be past when his works spoke for themselves, that is to say, for him. Hostility has already mounted, like a river in spate, so that he must conceal himself. Are we to see in this really a sign of failure, resignation before the relentless power of the contradiction he meets with? Matthew actually develops this question by means of the text from the prophet Isaiah.

. . .[17]in order that the words of the prophet Isaiah might be fulfilled, who said: [18]" Behold, my servant whom I have chosen, my beloved in whom my soul is well-pleased. I will put my Spirit upon him, and he will proclaim judgment to the nations. [19]He will not contend or cry out, and his voice will not be heard in the streets. [20]The bruised reed he will not break, and the flickering

wick he will not quench, till he has brought judgment to victory.
²¹And in his name shall the peoples hope."

St. Matthew gives only a few other Old Testament quotations
so fully. He thereby gives us a key to the understanding of the
Messiah. By the fact that he goes into concealment, even though
forced thereto from outside, the picture of the servant of God in
Isaiah is verified in him. God takes back none of the qualities
with which he has endowed his servant from the very beginning.
He has chosen him to be the Emmanuel (" God with us ") and
" to save his people from their sins " (1:21-23). He is " his beloved Son " in whom his soul is well-pleased as he revealed
himself at the baptism in the Jordan. There the Spirit was laid
upon him. He began to work mightily in him, beginning with
the struggle with Satan in the desert. Jesus' first utterance spoke
of the kingship in which the divine judgment was proclaimed:
" to the nations," according to Isaiah, therefore not only to
Israel! The prophet says that the words of the Messiah are meant
for all and will be delivered to the peoples of the earth. All this
has already been disclosed to us in many images.

But the prophet's knowledge is not confined to that call and its
brilliant inauguration. He looks into the future and sees that the
servant of God does not march out like a military leader or a
revolutionary who turns everything upside down. He recognizes
in him a deep inward activity which aims at healing and redres-
sing the roots of things. The servant does not contend or cry out,
nor does he fill the streets with the reverberation of his words.
His vocation is carefully and mercifully to raise up what is cast
down, to heal all wounds, to give heart to the discouraged, to
bend down to the sinner. There is no contention as happens
among us ordinary men, nor is there noisy debate in working

out the truth in common. Even when faced with his enemies Jesus does nothing but proclaim the judgment of God. We cannot make the gospel a subject of debate. All we can do is obey it. The object of all that we say about God's message is to stimulate each other to a more perfect obedience.

In obscurity, in this quiet and unostentatious work of salvation, Jesus fulfills the call of God. And yet this is the way of success for the plan which is that " judgment be brought to victory." It is not the justice on which we men insist, nor the justice that is embodied in the law, but God's justice, the right which he claims inexorably—the recognition of his majesty. In the name of the servant lies the hope of the nations, of all nations, including Israel. As the apostles had already been told, the way of the Messiah leads from lowliness to exaltation, from obscurity to light: " What I say to you in darkness, repeat in the light, and what you hear whispered in your ears, proclaim from the housetops " (10:27).

This way is also described by the evangelist John, only that he expands it in regard to the first movement from above to below. In John the way goes from the preëxistent Word of God, down through the lowliness of the flesh, and up again once more, by his exaltation to the Father: " I went forth from the Father and came into the world. I go out of the world again and go to the Father " (Jn. 16:28).

God or Satan (12:22–45)

The crisis reaches its climax in the following episodes. Here, as in the story of the temptation (4:5–11), the sharpness of the conflict is made clear. But it is no longer in the background in the invisible struggle between God and Satan; it is in the foreground, in the struggle between Jewish opposition and the Messiah of God. It begins with the renewed charge of a pact with the devil, followed by a long statement in which Jesus defends himself (12:22-37). Then comes a call to repentance with a judgment-saying condemning the hostile generation (12:38-42). The saying about relapse forms a menacing conclusion to the discourse (12:43-45).

KINGDOM OF GOD OR KINGDOM OF SATAN (12:22-37)

²²*Then a possessed man was brought to him, who was blind and dumb, and he healed him, so that the mute spoke and saw.* ²³*And all the crowds were beside themselves and said: " Is not this the Son of David?"* ²⁴*But the Pharisees heard it and said: " This man drives out demons only through Beelzebub, the prince of the demons."*

We have already read of one such similar episode (9:32-34). Once more there is someone possessed by a demon, once more the people break out into excited applause. In the previous case the crowd made the astonished observation that nothing of the sort had ever been experienced in Israel; here it goes so far as to ask: " Is not this the Son of David?" This is a step forward. " Son of David " is a designation of the Messiah. How close they seem to come to the truth! But it only seems to be so. For the contrast of the accusation stands out all the sharper: it is with the aid of the prince of demons that he drives out demons. It is one and the same event, but the verdict is different! What seems to some of them entirely hopeful, seems to others nothing but barefaced mass deception. Is it the work of God or is it Satan's sleight of hand? In God's government of the church two men

are constantly called upon to make such a decision. Only willing
and obedient faith can recognize that in it is attested not a human
art of seduction, but divine love.

*²⁵But he knew their thoughts and said to them: " Every king-
dom that is divided within itself will be laid waste, and every
city and every house that is divided within itself will not abide.
²⁶And if Satan drives out Satan, he is divided against himself.
How then can his kingdom abide? ²⁷And if I drive out demons
by Beelzebub, by whom do your sons drive them out? Therefore
these shall be your judges."*

The defense offered by the Lord is built in strict logical sequence.
The very sharpness of the argument is an expression of the irreconcilable opposition between kingdom of God and kingdom of
Satan. In the temptation, the evil one spoke only of the riches of
the world which he thought he could dispose of at choice (4:8).
Here Jesus himself speaks of Satan's kingdom. His rule is to be
compared with a state, or again with a city or house, in which
order reigns under the sway of authority. If a family is split within itself, the children revolt against their parents (10:34-36). A
civil war can bring down a whole kingdom; then all order
ceases to exist. Its power to maintain itself lies in unity, in the
collective effort of its many members towards a common end.
If one rises up against another, the pillars of good order collapse
and that is the end. The kingdom of Satan seems to be modeled
on the kingdom of God, indeed, seems to ape it. He has set up
an opposition government, a counterpart kingdom. Unity in
plenitude does not exist there as with God, but only a caricature
of it: everything serving the cause of evil must be twisted,
wounded, and split. On this point all the subjects of this

" realm " are united. How then can one be working against
another? How can Satan be committing suicide?

Jesus throws another argument into the discussion. Your own
sons, that is, your disciples, are in fact active as exorcists, driving
out demons. You yourselves have taught them how. They will
be your judges because they testify to me and my works, since
the evil one yields only to the power of God. They too can only
have success, in so far as they confront the demonic might in the
name of the Lord.

 ^{28}*" But if I by the Spirit of God drive out demons, then the
kingdom of God is already come upon you."*

Up to this we had razor-sharp proofs. Now comes, however, the
tremendous proclamation of Jesus to his works. Up to this,
reason was obliged to bow, now faith alone can grasp what is
said. It is not the spirit of the evil one; it is the Spirit of God that
works in me. It is through his power, with which I have been
anointed, that the demons are conquered. And when that takes
place, the kingship of God already arrives. When the powers of
evil are driven out, the lordship of God can march in. The space
for it to occupy is fought for yard by yard, and painfully. But
then it really comes about that the majesty of God triumphs.
Satan's realm does not collapse because of its own inner contradictions, but because of the greater power of the kingdom of
God. This is one of the most tremendous sayings of the gospel.
What power must be revealed where the Spirit of God works,
not only in the expulsion of an evil spirit as here, but in our
modest works also, when they are done " in the Spirit of God " :
in strong prayer, in humble service or even only in a good
thought or good wish for our fellow men.

²⁹" Or how can anyone break into the house of the strong one and rob his goods, if he has not bound the strong one beforehand? Only then can he despoil his house."

A small parable. The image is taken from war and is grim and realistic. To plunder someone's house and despoil him of his possessions you must first have fettered the enemy, the owner of the house, otherwise it will go hard with you. The householder receives the rather strange designation of " the strong one." This is understandable in the parable because the title is needed to bring out the danger which causes the robber so much trouble. But Jesus had been speaking of Satan and the parable is meant to carry on the thought of the preceding section. Satan is strong because he is at the head of a kingdom. Only someone stronger than he will overpower and fetter him if he wishes to despoil him of his goods. Who else can the stronger be but him whom John the Baptist had already announced in the words : " But he who comes after me is stronger than I " (3 : 11)? Yes, he is stronger even than Satan, and he alone will succeed in rendering him harmless. The demons flee before the might of his word, Satan suffers defeat after defeat. We are powerless when we count upon our own strength. Only the power of Jesus within us, the strong one, can master evil : which is hatred, the lie, and enmity against God.

³⁰" He that is not with me is against me, and he who does not gather with me, scatters."

God against Satan and the Messiah against Satan : that is one and the same thing. He who turns against Jesus, turns also against God. Jesus alone is equal to the power of the evil one because he is completely in God and God is entirely with him. Man's real decision is taken with regard to Jesus alone. And still more: He who does not cooperate actively with Jesus, like the disciples in his lifetime, is actually working against him, and scattering. The image implies that the work of Jesus is a gathering-in, a thought expressed for instance in the gathering of " the lost sheep of the house of Israel " (10:6). The picture of shepherd and flock rises up once more. The wolf breaking into the flock scatters it. We do not just take up a standpoint somewhere along the line; it is not a matter of a decision only taken once. This decision must be constantly realized and win concrete form in action. It cannot remain a theory, merely a spiritual attitude. It is only true and genuine where each day's effort is fed from it and that means: to gather with Jesus, to do his work of shepherd, to work for him.

[31]" Therefore I tell you: Every sin and every blasphemy will be forgiven men, but the blasphemy against the Spirit will not be forgiven. [32]And if anyone speaks a word against the Son of Man, it will be forgiven him; but whoever speaks against the Holy Spirit will not be forgiven, neither in this age of the world nor in the age to come."

Jesus speaks of a sin, that of blasphemy, of evil words about God. This sin is always directed against what is divine and sacred, in contradistinction to other sins which are directed against men and human values. Jesus distinguishes between blasphemy against the Holy Spirit and blasphemy against the Son of Man. It is hard to understand how the latter, the sin against the Son of Man, can be forgiven while the former cannot!

Jesus uses the title " Son of Man " when speaking of himself, but it is a name which hides his identity. It need mean no more than " man " but it can also imply the highest dignities : authority to forgive sin, the office of judge at the end of time. At any rate, he is outwardly a man like any other. One can be wrong about him, as this very episode shows. One can wilfully misinterpret his miracles, as has happened before (12:24). As a man among men, he is the object of conflict. Faith can be gained in his regard, but it can also be refused. This concealment of the divine fullness in human dress, this hiding of the divinity in weakness, can be reckoned to man as extenuating circumstances. He still has hope of forgiveness.

But whoever blasphemes against the Spirit of God knows exactly what he is doing. His attack is mounted directly against God. It is true than man can see neither God nor his Spirit, but man knows who he is. Whoever blasphemes God always means really God himself. There is no longer any twilight of doubt or uncertainty—and therefore likewise no excuse.

Jesus proclaims solemnly that it is in the Spirit of God that he drives out demons. Blasphemy against him is therefore in reality a blasphemy against the Spirit. And this sin cannot be forgiven because the blasphemer, so to speak, excludes himself from forgiveness. Neither here in the present age of the world, nor in the future age, can he receive pardon. He has separated himself from God.

[33]" *Either you think: the tree is good, then so too are its fruits good; or you think: the tree is evil, then so too are its fruits evil. For a tree is known by its fruits.* [34]*Brood of vipers! How can you speak good words since you are evil? For the mouth utters what the heart is full of.* [35]*The good man brings good things out of the good treasure, and the evil man brings evil things out of the evil treasure."*

Here the picture of the tree and its fruit is applied once more. He whose words are evil, whose utterances are filled with wickedness and hatred, can have no good heart. The whole man is darkened (see 6:22f.). The exterior renders faithfully the interior situation. Your wickedness of heart proclaims itself in your blasphemous speech. It testifies that you are thoroughly corrupt and that God is not in you. Just as the foul and rotten tree is recognized by its useless fruits, so too your wickedness by your speech.

Jesus once more uses the harsh form of address which the Baptist had already used: " You brood of vipers." Such wickedness is not always recognized at once. It is not bound to proclaim itself externally as malice. It is disguised under the cloak of piety and hides itself behind the avowed intention of serving God. It is hypocrisy such as Jesus had already reproached the Pharisees with in the Sermon on the Mount (6:1–18), and such as he will treat more fundamentally later on in the great discourse of " Woes " in chapter 23. The image of the tree is accompanied by the proverbial wisdom of experience: " For the mouth utters what the heart is full of." A man's sincerity and the clear transparency of his whole being must manifest themselves in his speech. It will be recognized there by those people who are sufficiently true and sincere to make out the real intention from the sound of the words they hear.

Thus man has in his heart a treasure which is either good and valuable, or evil and hollow. How close is the connection between what a man is and what he says, between the word of his lips and the constitution of his being. This is a truth which is also confirmed by our daily experience. In the long run one can recognize another from the inner sincerity of his speech; but we ourselves can also be known by others. The word reveals our person.

It comes from the center of our being and tries to find the way to the heart of him to whom we speak. The greater the unity between our mind and our speech, the deeper are we penetrated and molded by the truth of God. Here again the beatitude is true: " Blessed are the pure of heart, for they shall see God " (5 : 8).

[36]" *But I tell you: Every idle word that men speak they will have to account for on the day of judgment.* [37]*For according to your words shall you be acquitted and according to your words shall you be condemned.*"

Words must be managed carefully. They have a high dignity and bring out into the open the most precious thing that we have within us. That is why we must be careful not to employ idle words. We shall have to account for each of them on the day of judgment. This is a terrifying thought. Just as our deeds are weighed and measured, so too are our words. But since Jesus speaks so seriously about them, they cannot be just the everyday words without which life would be unthinkable—conversation about the events of the day, about joys and cares of the family, discussions about purchases and food and about everything else that our words have to deal with constantly and indeed necessarily. Idle words must therefore be such as do not spring from that inner truthfulness, words that are insincere and ambiguous, secretly or deliberately hypocritical and bereft of love. They are all the words about our fellow men that are mere gossip, words about current affairs and these evil times that are just useless complaint and unbridled chatter. These will be weighed by God. We should strive hard to make all our speech more and more at one with our minds, with a heart which throbs with the beat of love.

THE DEMAND FOR A SIGN, AND THE SIGN FOR PENANCE (12: 38-42)

[38]*Then some of the scribes and the Pharisees answered him and said: " Master, we should like to see a sign from you."* [39]*But he replied to them, saying: " A wicked and adulterous generation asks for a sign, but no other sign will be given it except the sign of the prophet Jonas.* [40]*For as Jonas was in the belly of the sea monster for three days and three nights, so too shall the Son of Man be in the heart of the earth for three days and three nights."*

Pharisees and scribes approach Jesus with a demand. They address him respectfully as Master. They would like to see a sign from him. What sort of a sign should that be? Has he not already given signs all along the way, especially in his miracles? Didn't God himself speak at the very beginning and give a sign at the baptism in the Jordan? But they want something else. Their request could be honestly intended like the inquiry made by John the Baptist (11:2f.) who had asked was Jesus really the Messiah. His opponents could mean the same thing here and ask for a convincing sign, an undeniably certain miracle.

The answer given by the Lord is also similar to that given to John. He does not tell the Baptist directly that he is the Messiah, but directs him to the way of faith which is to conclude to his person from his works. Here too, the opponents receive no direct answer. But Jesus' refusal is much sharper. Jesus sees something wrong in the very demand; they are up in arms against the plan of God. The prophets had often charged their forefathers with being an evil generation, incapable of doing good and therefore an adulterous generation which violated unceasingly the covenant of love which God had made.

So too it is with this generation of Jesus' contemporaries. It demands its own sign because it will not accept those already given by God. It tries to force God to bow to their will, instead of submitting to his. Hence no sign will be given. Satan in the desert had no success with his demands for miraculous signs. In the last resort it is he who is behind their desire. One often hears it said, Yes, if God worked a miracle I would believe. But all the signs that show us the way are already in place. The rebellious will demands new and different ones upon which we ourselves can pass judgment to see if they are adequate to attesting God.

Nevertheless, there will be a sign set up which is obscurely called the " sign of the prophet Jonas." It will not be given at once, as the doctors of the law demand, but at the moment God wills. It is the sign of Jesus' death and resurrection. Jonas was immured in the belly of the sea monster for three days as God's punishment for his disobedience. And then he was miraculously rescued and sent to preach to Nineveh. The Son of Man will be three days in the heart of the earth (that is, the underworld) in the fulfillment of his obedience. He dies the death of a prophet, but is raised up by God and exalted in glory. That is the sign which God will give—to the Jews a scandal, to the gentiles foolishness—a sign that will evoke contradiction. It pleased God, who had turned the wisdom of the world into folly, to save believers by the folly of the preaching (of the cross). This is how the apostle sees the sign of salvation which God sets up (1 Cor. 1:20–23). The temptation of demanding signs from God has often been felt in the course of church history. All those who demand special revelations, new miracles, secret instructions on events and dates, on wars and catastrophes, or the end of the world come under the same ban as the opponents

here. No sign will be given except the sign of the prophet Jonas.
Everything else is superstition or want of faith.

*41"The men of Nineveh shall appear at judgment with this
generation and condemn it; for they were converted by the
preaching of Jonas and behold, here is more than Jonas. 42The
queen of the South shall rise up at judgment with this generation
and condemn it; for she came from the ends of the earth to
hear the wisdom of Solomon, and behold, here is more than
Solomon."*

Two examples from sacred scripture are used to reinforce Jesus'
answer: this generation has already passed judgment upon
itself, it has no more signs to wait for. It was heathens that the
prophet Jonas had been sent to, heathens in a proverbially arro-
gant and dissolute city, Nineveh, the capital of the Assyrian
kingdom. A prophet was enough to bring it to repentance.
"Here is more than Jonas." The call to repentance has rung out
in vain, this generation refused to repent. Jesus had already told
the heathen centurion that he had found no such faith in Israel.
The heathens coming from the four corners of the earth will sit
down together at table along with Abraham, Isaac, and Jacob,
instead of the proper heirs (8:11-12). Here Jesus goes a step
further. The heathens will not only come in instead of Israel,
but in a process of law before the divine court of judgment they
will help to utter the condemnation of this generation!

The second example speaks also of a heathen, the queen of
Saba, the rich gold field of Arabia, who came to Solomon with
costly gifts in order to listen to his wisdom. She too will appear
as prosecutor on that day. Because no matter how enlightened
and wise Solomon was, here is more than he! These words

throw light on Jesus himself. He is a preacher of repentance like Jonas and the other prophets, but he is also teacher of the way of God like Solomon and all the teachers of wisdom after him. He is both prophet and teacher, and yet more than both.

Many men outside the church contemplate it with reverence and longing. Many accept its message, when it speaks of human dignity, peace and the unity of nations. Many see the " sign among the peoples " (Is. 11 : 12) even though they do not arrive at full knowledge of the truth. We may well ask will many of these not protest on the day of judgment against members of the church who possessed the truth and yet deep within them were unbelievers demanding signs and trying to force God's hand, but never repented?

WARNING AGAINST RELAPSING (12:43–45)

⁴³" But when the unclean spirit departs from man, he wanders through waterless regions seeking a resting place, but does not find it. ⁴⁴Then he says: ' I will return to the house from which I departed.' And he comes and finds it empty, swept out and decorated. ⁴⁵Then he goes and brings with him seven other spirits who are worse than he and they enter and dwell there. And the last state of that man will be worse than the first. So too shall it be with this wicked generation."

Once more the picture of the desert is conjured up. The bare steppe, its withered, lifeless monotony, seems sinister to the inhabitant of the fertile cultivated land. The desert seems to besiege him like a dangerous enemy. It is the dwelling place of the demons. There too Jesus had fought with Satan. From their home in the desert they press forward into the realm of men and try to make themselves at home there. When they are driven out—as always happened by the power of the word of Jesus— then they have nothing else to do than return to their desert home, which is in fact homelessness.

But it may also happen that the evil one is forcibly driven out of a man; but that this man did not inwardly renounce him. On the contrary, the occupying power, the dark spirit, was pleasing to him. Now he remains empty because the fullness of God has not occupied the space left free. He is still always ready inwardly to receive the evil guest, indeed he actually longs for him and entices him in. If the demon, prowling around, comes near by, then " he finds the house unoccupied, swept out and decorated." That must excite him once more and fill him with truly satanic joy. He goes and gathers comrades and with them he enters the house again, the heart of the man. There they can bustle around and do their evil business and make the man even more unhappy than he was before.

It is a strange world which is opened up to us by this saying, and one thought out entirely in terms of the ideas of Jesus' contemporaries. But in and through all these curious notions we can see perfectly well what is really at stake: the decision for or against God which is made in the heart (" the house "). It corresponds to what each of us can imagine as a terrifying example. A man who has once renounced evil is much worse off when he relapses into it a second time.

But it is only an example. What the Lord really means to say is contained in the last sentence: " So too shall it be with this wicked generation." Jesus regards the mass of his opponents as such backsliders. Perhaps at the beginning they partly believed his word, at least had a ready and open mind for him or even actually had begun the new life—it is not clear in detail. Perhaps we should look further back into the history of the people which was a story of repentance followed by constantly repeated apostasy. Since they allowed evil to master them so often in spite of all the passionate efforts of God, they are *recidivi,* sinners who always relapse, a truly " wicked race." Just as the man in the story at once renews his pact with the evil one, so too no real repentance has taken place in this generation. It will go worse with them than with any previous generation since truly here is " more than Jonas " and " more than Solomon."

The True Relatives of Jesus (12:46–50)

This episode concludes the great controversy with Jesus' opponents with a very significant point. The last word is not the threat uttered against the " wicked generation," but the reference to a counterpart, to a new generation which is truly dedicated to God.

[46]*While he was still speaking to the crowds, behold, his mother and his brothers appeared outside and sought to speak to him.* [47]*And someone said to him: " Behold, your mother and your brothers are outside and seek to speak to you." * [48]*But he answered the man who told him, saying: " Who is my mother, and who are my brothers?" * [49]*And he stretched out his hand over his disciples and said: " Behold, my mother and my brothers. * [50]*For whoever does the will of my Father in heaven, he is to me brother and sister and mother."*

Jesus speaks directly to the messenger who brought the news that his relatives wanted to speak with him—first putting a surprising question: " Who is my mother, and who are my brothers?" The question shows that Jesus has in mind something special. For after all, everyone knows who are his own mother and brothers. Nor does Jesus wish to assert that he has sundered himself from his mother Mary and his other relatives, as if he no longer regarded or knew them as blood relations and felt himself distant from them. The point is something different.

The evangelist says solemnly that Jesus stretched out his hand over his disciples. This is the gesture of taking possession, an expression of the fact that they belong to him, and also a sign of blessing. " *His disciples* " is what we read, not, for instance, " his apostles." The gesture is not restricted to the circle of the twelve, but embraces everybody who is interiorly in the relationship of disciple to the master, everybody who follows him. Of these all he says : " Behold, my mother and my brothers."

There is indeed a way to know the disciple of Jesus : it is the real fulfillment of the will of God. Anyone who bears this mark is at once the spiritual kin of Jesus : he is brother and sister and mother to Jesus. The bonds of blood, the natural relationship of family and race, the national unity, are not decisive for the kingship of God. Cutting across all these links, no matter how primordial and powerful, comes the exigent claim of the living God. He is the crossroads at which relatives and strangers, kinsmen and outsiders separate from one another. Had we not already heard that the word of Jesus can penetrate like a sword into the innermost circle of the family, and there part parents and children, daughter and mother, son and father (10 : 34–36); and that the obligation to Jesus must take precedence of obligation to father and mother (10 : 37)?

This is therefore the hallmark of the message of Jesus : the will of God is the supreme law, and this is what is decisive for discipleship and for really belonging to Jesus. For the Jews, this is important. They cannot appeal to God and God's will against the teaching of Jesus. It holds good also for Christians. They cannot use their profession of faith in Christ to absolve themselves from the active fulfillment of the will of God.

We heard that the disciple is not above the master, that the relationship of disciple to master, that is, of subordination and superiority, will never be set aside (10:24f.). Now something new is added to this. The disciple is a relative of Jesus in the spiritual sense. This relationship is also marked by warmth and familiarity. It does not stay within the bounds of obedience, subjection, and unconditional imitation. Rather, whoever gives himself to Jesus without reserve is adopted into his family. He comes close to Jesus and becomes familiar with him, like brothers and sisters, parents and children, living at home with one another. This is something consoling and beautiful. How many have found out by experience that among the brothers of Jesus there can be friendship much more intimate and rich than in natural relationship. The warmth and cordiality that exists between the disciples and their Master also permeates their relationship with one another. The kingship of God creates a new order of things, a spiritual union perceptible in faith, which surpasses by far all earthly bonds, though without lessening the value of family, race, and nation. However, in the new kinship, the spiritual membership of the church, we have already a foretaste of the full achievement to come. In every group in the church one can happily experience this, especially among those who in the literal sense also, have left all and followed Jesus.